let's talk science

Adventures in Creation

level I

Carrie Lindquist

MASTER BOOKS
— CURRICULUM —

Author: Carrie Linquist

Master Books Creative Team:

Editor: Laura Welch

Design: Diana Bogardus

Cover Design: Diana Bogardus

Copy Editors:
Judy Lewis
Willow Meek

Curriculum Review:
Laura Welch
Kristen Pratt
Diana Bogardus

First printing: August 2019
Fourth printing: August 2020

Master Books®, P.O. Box 726, Green Forest, AR 72638
Master Books® is a division of the New Leaf Publishing Group, Inc.

ISBN: 978-1-68344-174-8
ISBN: 978-1-61458-720-0 (digital)

Cover & Interior design by Diana Bogardus

All Scripture quotations, unless otherwise indicated, are taken from the Holy Bible, New International Version®, NIV®. Copyright ©1973, 1978, 1984, 2011 by Biblica, Inc.™ Used by permission of Zondervan. All rights reserved worldwide. www.zondervan.com The "NIV" and "New International Version" are trademarks registered in the United States Patent and Trademark Office by Biblica, Inc.™

Scripture quotations marked (NIrV) are taken from the Holy Bible, New International Reader's Version®, NIrV® Copyright © 1995, 1996, 1998, 2014 by Biblica, Inc.™ Used by permission of Zondervan. All rights reserved worldwide. www.zondervan.com The "NIrV" and "New International Reader's Version" are trademarks registered in the United States Patent and Trademark Office by Biblica, Inc.™

Printed in the United States of America.

Please visit our website for other great titles: www.masterbooks.com

About the Author

Carrie Lindquist is a homeschool graduate, wife to Wayne, and momma to two energetic boys. She is a passionate advocate for homeschooling and loves helping new-to-homeschooling moms to realize that homeschooling through the early years isn't scary — it's really just an extension of all the fun things they are already doing with their children! When she isn't cleaning the endless little messes her boys create, you can find her encouraging moms to embrace the calling of everyday faithfulness.

Table of Contents

Course Description

Approximately 20 minutes per lesson, three times per week

Designed for first graders in a one-year course

Let's Talk Science: Adventures in Creation will bring the Bible to life and instill in your child a love for science as they explore the world around them. Students will embark on an adventure through the days of creation as they discover that science is a wonderful tool God has given us to study His creation — and learn more about Him!

Through hands-on investigations and biblically inspired stories, students will experience, ask questions, and explore God's world through science. Students will use their imaginations to join Adam and Eve as they teach their children about God's creation, learn about the amazing things and creatures God created on each day of creation, engage in experiments and activities to bring learning to life, and compile a Science Notebook to share what they've learned about God and His world with others.

Course Objectives

Students completing this course will:

- Learn that the study of science starts with the Bible

- Explore the days of creation and learn about the amazing things God designed on each day

- Discover that science teaches many lessons about God and about our relationship with Him

- Develop a love for science through hands-on exploration and experimentation

- Compile a Science Notebook as they document their discoveries and share what they've learned with others

Course Overview

Lessons follow a weekly pattern of:

Learn

Day 1: Learn about the topic

Experience

Day 2: Experience the topic through experiments, investigations, or hands-on activities

Share

Day 3: Share what they've learned with others as they add a new page to their Science Notebook

A note from the author

Welcome to *Let's Talk Science: Adventures in Creation!* If your child is anything like my children, he or she asks many, many questions each day. Who made the world? How are clouds made? How do fish breathe? Why does it rain? Each question sparked by curiosity becomes an amazing opportunity to learn, discover, and explore.

It may surprise you to learn that science wasn't my favorite subject as a child. I found it to be a series of dry facts that I couldn't relate to. However, as my sons and I have sought answers to their questions, science has become our favorite subject. Each question presents an opportunity to explore God's designs in creation and to learn more about who He is.

Science is an amazing tool God has given us to learn about and explore the world He created. When we study God's creation through science, we see His creativity, organization, grace, and majesty on display. Of course, sometimes science also reminds us that the world was broken through sin, and there we find His mercy and a reminder that we all need Jesus.

This course is inspired by the questions my sons have asked and the adventures we've had as we've answered those questions. *Let's Talk Science: Adventures in Creation* is designed to be interactive, hands-on, easy to prepare for, and a lot of fun. This course is also designed to encourage curiosity. If your child is particularly interested in a topic or question, I invite you to spend some time exploring God's world together through books, videos, and resources. Make this course your own and have fun!

When my sons started school, each picked out a special 3-ring binder to hold their completed worksheets. One night after dinner, they excitedly brought out their binders to show Dad all the things they had learned that day. This quickly became a favorite part of our nightly routine and is the inspiration behind the student's Science Notebook in this course. Encourage your student to pick out their own binder or decorate it. It will be a very special part of their science adventure.

It is my prayer that as your child completes this course, they will discover a love for the amazing world of science and that what they learn draws their hearts closer to their Creator.

Course Components

Imagine That!: Historical fiction is used as a tool in Adventures in Creation to illustrate concepts, help students develop their reading skills, encourage further discussion, and as an opportunity to help students see Adam, Eve, Cain, and Abel as real people in history. While we don't know what their lives looked like beyond what the Bible tells us, we can imagine what their lives may have been like based on the details the Bible does provide.

Each story in *Adventures in Creation* is carefully introduced as something we are imagining together based on the lives of very real people in the Bible. Your student may recognize that Cain killed Abel when they were grown. The final lesson in this course mentions Cain's decision to disobey God's directions; however, any further explanation is left to the discretion of the parent.

At some point in time, Cain did make a choice, or series of choices, to allow anger and bitterness to dwell and grow in his heart — even to the point of ignoring God's direct warning that "sin is crouching at the door" (Genesis 4:7). Sin is always a sad thing. It separates us from God and it always hurts both ourselves and other people. Throughout these stories you'll find the theme of our choices. Young or old, we all have choices to make in our lives. These choices will either draw us closer to God or pull our hearts further and further away from Him.

These stories may also provide conversation starters as your student learns how to discern fact from fiction — a skill they will use throughout their whole life. You can read Adam, Eve, Cain, and Abel's full story in Genesis chapters 1-4 and talk with your student about what their lives may have looked like, how choices affect both our lives and the lives of others, and about God's plan of salvation through Jesus who paid the ultimate price for our sin.

The stories also feature many simple words. If your student is reading, or learning to read, ask them to help you read this section.

Discussion Starters: Discussion Starters at the end of the lesson provide additional questions, activities, or ideas to dive deeper into the topic. Questions for the student are included in speech bubbles. Additional activity ideas or tips are in orange text.

Let's Memorize: Many lessons feature a memory verse with accompanying hand motions. Hand motions are a great way to help your student memorize the verse! You may also customize or create your own motions.

Science Notebook: The student will compile a Science Notebook as he or she completes the course. Each week, the student will tear out the activity page on Day 3 and add that page to his or her Science Notebook to document what he or she learned. These pages are designated by a "Tear out for Science Notebook" note on the right-hand side of the page. Encourage your student to show someone else the page and share what he or she has learned during the week.

Flashlight	✓
Tissue paper or cellophane in colors: red, orange, yellow, green, and blue	☐
Rubber bands	☐
Crayons or colored pencils	☐

Weekly materials list

Materials List: Weekly hands-on activities are integral to this course. A Master Materials List (page 8) provides an at-a-glance view of the materials your student will need to complete the activities for each week. The activities are designed to be easy to prepare for, and most require materials you may already have on hand.

At the start of each week's lessons you'll find the Weekly Materials List included in the lesson. These are the materials you'll need to have on hand to complete activities and worksheets for the week.

The Materials Needed list shows the materials you'll need to complete that individual lesson.

Recommended Resources from Master Books®:

When You See a Rainbow, Aquarium Guide, Created Cosmos (DVD)

Helpful Tips

- Teacher tips and instructions are included in orange text.

- Some activities require cutting out components with scissors. As cutting abilities can vary greatly at this age, either the teacher or the student may cut these out.

- It is recommended to look through the Master Materials List before beginning this course and purchase any less common materials (such as a glass prism and/or magnifying glass) that are not already on hand.

- Your student may enjoy going shopping to pick out a special 3-ring binder for their Science Notebook.

- Lessons may inspire your student to ask additional questions or spark a desire to explore a topic deeper. Have fun researching together to find the answer, or spend some time on an off day exploring a topic in greater detail.

- This course is designed to be interactive with your student. Be sure to take time to pause after questions in the text and explore the topic with your student.

- If your student is reading or learning to read, encourage him or her to help you read the biblically inspired stories. The stories feature many short, simple words for emergent readers. As you read the stories together, point out words your student can read.

Master Materials List

Week 1

- [ ] 3-ring binder for student's Science Notebook
- [ ] Small rock or pebble, non-porous so it will sink in water
- [ ] Container of water to drop the rock into
- [ ] Crayons or colored pencils

Week 2

- [ ] Flashlight

Week 3

- [ ] White sheet of paper
- [ ] Glass prism (A glass prism will create a more vibrant rainbow and is recommended; however, an acrylic prism may also be used.)
- [ ] Light source — natural light outside or through a window is best, but a flashlight will also work.

Week 4

- [ ] Flashlight
- [ ] Tissue paper or cellophane in colors: red, orange, yellow, green, and blue
- [ ] Rubber bands (Optional, to hold tissue paper/cellophane in place on the flashlight. You can also simply use your hand.)
- [ ] Crayons, markers, or colored pencils

Week 5

Option A (recommended) — Outdoor Rainbow

- [ ] Garden hose with nozzle that allows mist
- [ ] Water source for hose
- [ ] Sunny day
- [ ] Optional: Paper, crayons, and surface to draw on

Option B — Indoor Rainbow

- [ ] Drinking glass, smooth glass is the best
- [ ] Water
- [ ] White sheet of paper
- [ ] Flashlight
- [ ] DVD or CD

Week 6

- [ ] Crayons

Week 7

- [ ] Glue stick
- [ ] Crayons, colored pencils, or markers
- [ ] Scissors

Week 8

- [ ] Glass cup
- [ ] Water
- [ ] Ice cubes
- [ ] Second small cup or bowl of water
- [ ] Paintbrush (or child's fingers will work)
- [ ] Dark-colored construction paper

Week 9

- [ ] Mason jar (recommended) or tall glass
- [ ] Lid for mason jar (recommended) or small saucer to cover glass
- [ ] Hot water (Hot tap water will do. If you do not see a cloud form, you may also run water through a coffee maker. Remind young children to be careful and not touch.)
- [ ] Aerosol spray (hairspray works well)
- [ ] 2–6 ice cubes
- [ ] Elmer's glue®
- [ ] Glue stick
- [ ] Cotton balls

Week 10

- [ ] Mason jar or large glass cup
- [ ] Shaving cream
- [ ] Blue food coloring
- [ ] Water
- [ ] Small bowl
- [ ] Dropper or spoon
- [ ] Plastic bag or a flat plate (to protect surface)

Week 11

- [ ] Balloon
- [ ] Fork
- [ ] Fleece (optional)

Week 12

- [ ] Crayons, colored pencils, or markers

Week 13

- [ ] Playdough in 4 colors
- [ ] Butter knife
- [ ] Glue stick
- [ ] Scissors

Week 14

- [ ] Stalks of celery, with leaves
- [ ] Glass jar
- [ ] Food coloring
- [ ] Water
- [ ] Scissors

Week 15

- [ ] Magnifying glass
- [ ] Various leaves from outside. May also use spinach or leaves from grocery store flowers.
- [ ] Paper
- [ ] Crayons

Week 16

- [ ] Flour
- [ ] Cheetos®
- [ ] Cocoa powder
- [ ] Light, fuzzy winter gloves
- [ ] 3 pieces of construction paper
- [ ] Crayons or markers
- [ ] Pom-poms
- [ ] Elmer's glue®

Week 17

- [ ] Apple
- [ ] Cutting board
- [ ] Sharp knife — adult only!

Week 18

- [ ] Paper plate
- [ ] Red, orange, and yellow tissue paper or construction paper, cut or torn into approximately 1-inch pieces
- [ ] Glue stick

Week 19

- [ ] Paper plate sun from week 18
- [ ] String or yarn, 4–5 feet long
- [ ] Elmer's glue®

Week 20

- [ ] Flour or playdough
- [ ] Container
- [ ] Small objects such as pebbles or marbles to drop into the flour or playdough
- [ ] White paint
- [ ] Black construction paper
- [ ] Cotton ball
- [ ] Pencil
- [ ] Optional: Clothespin for less mess. Use the clothespin to hold the cotton ball, and the student can hold onto the top of the clothespin.
- [ ] Hole punch

Week 21

Option A:
- [ ] Oreos™

Option B:
- [ ] Flashlight
- [ ] Ball, such as a tennis or soccer ball

Week 22

- [ ] 6 popsicle sticks
- [ ] Glue
- [ ] String or yarn
- [ ] Optional: Silver or gold glitter

Week 23

- [ ] Cardstock or index card
- [ ] Pushpin or pencil
- [ ] Flashlight

Week 24

- [ ] Magnifying glass
- [ ] Feathers (can be purchased at a craft store or gathered from the yard)
- [ ] Velcro (can be on an article of clothing or a shoe)
- [ ] Elmer's glue®

Week 25

Option A:
- [ ] Toilet paper or paper towel cardboard roll, or a pinecone
- [ ] Peanut butter
- [ ] Birdseed
- [ ] Yarn or twine
- [ ] Plate
- [ ] Butter knife

Option B:
- [ ] Needle and thread
- [ ] Unbuttered, unsalted popcorn
- [ ] Apples and oranges, cut into pieces
- [ ] Berries, if desired

Week 26

- [ ] Yarn or twine
- [ ] Cotton balls
- [ ] Large container for student to build a nest
- [ ] Dried grass, twigs, etc., that the student has gathered from outside
- [ ] Glue stick
- [ ] Scissors

Week 27

- [ ] Mason jar or big glass container
- [ ] Glass container for mixing
- [ ] Funnels
- [ ] Syringe (one from a child's liquid medicine will work well)
- [ ] Corn syrup
- [ ] Water
- [ ] Vegetable oil
- [ ] Blue food coloring
- [ ] Dark blue dish soap
- [ ] Rubbing alcohol
- [ ] 1/2 or 1/4 measuring cup, depending on the size of your jar

Week 28

- [ ] Sink or bathtub full of water
- [ ] Fork
- [ ] Spoon
- [ ] Construction paper
- [ ] Scissors
- [ ] Elmer's glue® or glue stick
- [ ] Crayons or markers
- [ ] Glitter (optional)

Week 29

- [ ] Clear 1-liter soda bottle
- [ ] Glow stick bracelet or glow in the dark paint
- [ ] Construction paper
- [ ] Permanent marker
- [ ] Scissors
- [ ] Tape

Week 30

- [ ] Scissors
- [ ] Glue stick

Week 31

- [ ] Container to hold habitat
- [ ] Animal toys belonging to one habitat your student chooses: arctic, rain forest, forest, or desert
- [ ] Materials to build a habitat for the toys (e.g., ice for arctic, sand for desert, etc.)

Week 32

- [ ] Two straws
- [ ] Tape or rubber bands
- [ ] 2 paper bags or gallon-sized Ziploc® bags

Week 33

- [ ] Soda bottle
- [ ] Straw
- [ ] Playdough
- [ ] Water

Week 34

- [ ] Balloon
- [ ] Ink pad
- [ ] Picture of student
- [ ] Glue Sticks

Week 35

- [ ] Ice cube made from fruit juice
- [ ] Plate

Week 36

- [ ] Scissors
- [ ] Glue stick

Schedule

Date	Day	Assignment	Due Date	✓
Week 1	Day ●	Read and complete Day 1 • How We Study Science • Pages 17–21		
	Day ●●	Read and complete Day 2 • How We Study Science • Pages 22–24		
	Day ●●●	Read and complete Day 3 • How We Study Science • Pages 25–26		
Week 2	Day ●	Read and complete Day 1 • The First Day of Creation • Pages 27–29		
	Day ●●	Read and complete Day 2 • The First Day of Creation • Pages 30–32		
	Day ●●●	Read and complete Day 3 • The First Day of Creation • Pages 33–34		
Week 3	Day ●	Read and complete Day 1 • Light Is Made of Colors • Pages 35–37		
	Day ●●	Read and complete Day 2 • Light Is Made of Colors • Pages 38–40		
	Day ●●●	Read and complete Day 3 • Light Is Made of Colors • Pages 41–42		
Week 4	Day ●	Read and complete Day 1 • Light Waves • Pages 43–46		
	Day ●●	Read and complete Day 2 • Light Waves • Pages 47–48		
	Day ●●●	Read and complete Day 3 • Light Waves • Pages 49–50		
Week 5	Day ●	Read and complete Day 1 • Rainbows • Pages 51–53		
	Day ●●	Read and complete Day 2 • Rainbows • Pages 54-56		
	Day ●●●	Read and complete Day 3 • Rainbows • Pages 57-58		
Week 6	Day ●	Read and complete Day 1 • The Second Day of Creation • Pages 59–62		
	Day ●●	Read and complete Day 2 • The Second Day of Creation • Pages 63–64		
	Day ●●●	Read and complete Day 3 • The Second Day of Creation • Pages 65–66		
Week 7	Day ●	Read and complete Day 1 • Atmosphere • Pages 67–70		
	Day ●●	Read and complete Day 2 • Atmosphere • Pages 70–74		
	Day ●●●	Read and complete Day 3 • Atmosphere • Pages 74–76		
Week 8	Day ●	Read and complete Day 1 • Condensation and Evaporation • Pages 77–80		
	Day ●●	Read and complete Day 2 • Condensation and Evaporation • Pages 80–82		
	Day ●●●	Read and complete Day 3 • Condensation and Evaporation • Pages 83–84		
Week 9	Day ●	Read and complete Day 1 • Clouds • Pages 85–88		
	Day ●●	Read and complete Day 2 • Clouds • Pages 89–90		
	Day ●●●	Read and complete Day 3 • Clouds • Pages 90–91		

Schedule

Date	Day	Assignment	Due Date	✓
Week 10	Day	Read and complete Day 1 • The Water Cycle • Pages 93–97		
	Day	Read and complete Day 2 • The Water Cycle • Page 98		
	Day	Read and complete Day 3 • The Water Cycle • Pages 99–100		
Week 11	Day	Read and complete Day 1 • Thunderstorms • Pages 101-104		
	Day	Read and complete Day 2 • Thunderstorms • Pages 105–107		
	Day	Read and complete Day 3 • Thunderstorms • Pages 108–110		
Week 12	Day	Read and complete Day 1 • The Third Day of Creation • Pages 111–114		
	Day	Read and complete Day 2 • The Third Day of Creation • Pages 115–118		
	Day	Read and complete Day 3 • The Third Day of Creation • Pages 119–120		
Week 13	Day	Read and complete Day 1 • Earth Layers • Pages 121–124		
	Day	Read and complete Day 2 • Earth Layers • Pages 125-127		
	Day	Read and complete Day 3 • Earth Layers • Pages 129–130		
Week 14	Day	Read and complete Day 1 • Plants • Pages 131–136		
	Day	Read and complete Day 2 • Plants • Pages 137–139		
	Day	Read and complete Day 3 • Plants • Pages 140–142		
Week 15	Day	Read and complete Day 1 • Leaves and Photosynthesis • Pages 143–146		
	Day	Read and complete Day 2 • Leaves and Photosynthesis • Pages 146–148		
	Day	Read and complete Day 3 • Leaves and Photosynthesis • Pages 149–150		
Week 16	Day	Read and complete Day 1 • Flowers and Pollination • Pages 151–155		
	Day	Read and complete Day 2 • Flowers and Pollination • Pages 156-158		
	Day	Read and complete Day 3 • Flowers and Pollination • Page 159		
Week 17	Day	Read and complete Day 1 • Seeds • Pages 161–164		
	Day	Read and complete Day 2 • Seeds • Pages 165–166		
	Day	Read and complete Day 3 • Seeds • Pages 167–168		
Week 18	Day	Read and complete Day 1 • The Fourth Day of Creation • Pages 169–174		
	Day	Read and complete Day 2 • The Fourth Day of Creation • Pages 175–176		
	Day	Read and complete Day 3 • The Fourth Day of Creation • Pages 177–178		

Schedule

Date	Day	Assignment	Due Date	✓
Week 19	Day	Read and complete Day 1 • Sun • Pages 179–181		
	Day	Read and complete Day 2 • Sun • Pages 182–184		
	Day	Read and complete Day 3 • Sun • Page 185		
Week 20	Day	Read and complete Day 1 • Moon — Surface • Pages 187–192		
	Day	Read and complete Day 2 • Moon — Surface • Pages 193–194		
	Day	Read and complete Day 3 • Moon — Surface • Pages 195–196		
Week 21	Day	Read and complete Day 1 • Moon — Phases • Pages 197–201		
	Day	Read and complete Day 2 • Moon — Phases • Pages 202-204		
	Day	Read and complete Day 3 • Moon — Phases • Pages 205–206		
Week 22	Day	Read and complete Day 1 • Stars • Pages 207–211		
	Day	Read and complete Day 2 • Stars • Page 212		
	Day	Read and complete Day 3 • Stars • Pages 213–214		
Week 23	Day	Read and complete Day 1 • Constellations • Pages 215–219		
	Day	Read and complete Day 2 • Constellations • Pages 220–222		
	Day	Read and complete Day 3 • Constellations • Pages 223–224		
Week 24	Day	Read and complete Day 1 • The Fifth Day of Creation • Pages 225–228		
	Day	Read and complete Day 2 • The Fifth Day of Creation • Pages 229–230		
	Day	Read and complete Day 3 • The Fifth Day of Creation • Page 231		
Week 25	Day	Read and complete Day 1 • Birds • Pages 233–235		
	Day	Read and complete Day 2 • Birds • Pages 236-237		
	Day	Read and complete Day 3 • Birds • Pages 238–240		
Week 26	Day	Read and complete Day 1 • Bird Nests • Pages 241–244		
	Day	Read and complete Day 2 • Bird Nests • Pages 245–246		
	Day	Read and complete Day 3 • Bird Nests • Pages 247–250		
Week 27	Day	Read and complete Day 1 • Layers of the Ocean • Pages 251–254		
	Day	Read and complete Day 2 • Layers of the Ocean • Pages 255–256		
	Day	Read and complete Day 3 • Layers of the Ocean • Pages 257–259		

Schedule

Date	Day	Assignment	Due Date	✓
Week 28	Day 1	Read and complete Day 1 • The Sunlit and Twilight Ocean Zones • Pages 261–265		
	Day 2	Read and complete Day 2 • The Sunlit and Twilight Ocean Zones • Pages 266–267		
	Day 3	Read and complete Day 3 • The Sunlit and Twilight Ocean Zones • Pages 268–269		
Week 29	Day 1	Read and complete Day 1 • Deep-sea Creatures • Pages 271–275		
	Day 2	Read and complete Day 2 • Deep-sea Creatures • Page 276		
	Day 3	Read and complete Day 3 • Deep-sea Creatures • Pages 277–278		
Week 30	Day 1	Read and complete Day 1 • The Sixth Day of Creation • Pages 279–284		
	Day 2	Read and complete Day 2 • The Sixth Day of Creation • Page 284		
	Day 3	Read and complete Day 3 • The Sixth Day of Creation • Pages 285-288		
Week 31	Day 1	Read and complete Day 1 • Animal Habitats • Pages 289–293		
	Day 2	Read and complete Day 2 • Animal Habitats • Page 294		
	Day 3	Read and complete Day 3 • Animal Habitats • Pages 295–296		
Week 32	Day 1	Read and complete Day 1 • Mankind • Pages 297-301		
	Day 2	Read and complete Day 2 • Mankind • Pages 302–304		
	Day 3	Read and complete Day 3 • Mankind • Pages 305–306		
Week 33	Day 1	Read and complete Day 1 • The Circulatory System • Pages 307–312		
	Day 2	Read and complete Day 2 • The Circulatory System • Pages 313–314		
	Day 3	Read and complete Day 3 • The Circulatory System • Pages 315–316		
Week 34	Day 1	Read and complete Day 1 • Uniquely You • Pages 317–321		
	Day 2	Read and complete Day 2 • Uniquely You • Page 322		
	Day 3	Read and complete Day 3 • Uniquely You • Pages 323–324		
Week 35	Day 1	Read and complete Day 1 • The Five Senses • Pages 325–328		
	Day 2	Read and complete Day 2 • The Five Senses • Pages 329–330		
	Day 3	Read and complete Day 3 • The Five Senses • Pages 331–332		
Week 36	Day 1	Read and complete Day 1 • Conclusion • Pages 333–338		
	Day 2	Read and complete Day 2 • Conclusion • Pages 338–342		
	Day 3	Read and complete Day 3 • Conclusion • Pages 343–345		

Image Credit

How We Study Science

Day

Learn

Welcome to our science adventure. I'm so excited to explore God's incredible creation with you! Wait, what was that you asked? What is science? Well, that is a really great question. Let's talk about it!

Science is an amazing tool God has given us to learn about and explore the world He created. Science helps us ask questions, test our ideas, and share what we learn about the world and about God with others. Science helps us learn more about God — who He is and what He does.

So how do we study science? Well, first we start with the Bible. The Bible is God's Word to us, and we begin to study science through it. You see, God created everything — and when we wonder about something in His creation, He is the first one we should ask!

The Bible tells us God created the heavens and the earth and everything in them! As our Creator, He understands everything and knows exactly how each area of creation works and fits together.

Psalm 111:2–4 tells us, *"Great are the works of the LORD; they are pondered by all who delight in them. Glorious and majestic are his deeds, and his righteousness endures forever. He has caused his wonders to be remembered; the LORD is gracious and compassionate."*

When we study God's creation through science, we see His creativity, organization, grace, mercy, and majesty on display in everything.

In the Bible, we learn that God created the first two people, Adam and Eve. They were real people — just like us! God placed them in a beautiful garden. Do you remember the name of the garden?

It was the Garden of Eden. It was a perfect place where God walked and talked with Adam and Eve! Can you imagine what it would have been like to walk and talk with God? The Bible doesn't tell us all the things God may have talked about with Adam and Eve — we can imagine what they may have talked about, though.

But then, something terrible happened. Adam and Eve disobeyed God's directions. They did something wrong. They sinned, and sin separates us from God. Because of their sin, Adam and Eve had to leave the Garden of Eden. Their sin broke the world. It was no longer perfect as God had created it to be — and one day, they would die.

After they left the Garden of Eden, Adam and Eve had children — boys and girls, just like you! The Bible tells us some of their names were Cain, Abel, and later Seth. I'm sure their children asked Adam and Eve many questions — just like you ask me — and Adam and Eve likely taught their children the things God had taught them.

We can use our imagination to think of things they may have talked about together! Maybe one night, their talk went something like this . . .

Weekly materials list

Material	
3-ring binder for student's Science Notebook	✓
Small rock or pebble, non-porous so it will sink in water	☐
Container of water to drop the rock into	☐
Crayons or colored pencils	☐

Teacher tip: The story passages are designed with many short, simple words. If your student is learning to read or reading fluently, you can direct him or her to read the words that are at their reading level. You can also preview the text and highlight or underline words they can read. Once your student has read the word, continue reading to them until you reach the next word they can read.

Bible-inspired stories

It was a still night. The stars were bright in the sky.

"Dad?"

"Yes, Abel?" Adam said.

"Can you tell me again? Can you tell me how God made the world? I want to know all about it."

"Yes, son. I would love to!" Adam was quiet for a minute as he thought back to the days he walked and talked with God. He remembered asking God that same question, "How did you make the world?" and God had told him.

"Well, Abel, at the start there was nothing. But God was there. He had always been there, and He always will be there. At the start, there was no world, no plants, no animals. There was nothing, then God started creating. First, God created the heavens and the earth — but it was empty and dark. Then, God just spoke! He said, 'Let there be light!' and then there was light!"

"Did you ask God about the earth and light, Dad?"

"I did son, and God told me many things about them! Would you like to learn them?"

"Yes, please!"

Adam smiled. "It is getting late. We should go to sleep. But when we wake up in the morning, I'll tell you all about God's creation."

"Okay, Dad, I am very excited to learn about God's creation!"

name

I'm so very excited to learn about God's creation with you, too! Let's read Psalm 111:2–4 once more: *"Great are the works of the LORD; they are pondered by all who delight in them. Glorious and majestic are his deeds, and his righteousness endures forever. He has caused his wonders to be remembered; the LORD is gracious and compassionate."*

Color a picture of the earth, one of God's great works!

Discussion Starters ►

What is science?

What do we start with when we learn about science?

Let's memorize

Psalm 111:2

"**Great** are the **works** of the **LORD**; they are **pondered** by **all** who **delight** in them."

	Actions
Great	Place both hands in front of you over your head. Palms will face out like they would in a "stop" signal.
works	Make your hands into fists — one on the bottom, one on top. Tap your top fist onto the bottom fist.
LORD	Make an L with your pointer finger and thumb on your left hand. Place your L hand at your right shoulder and cross it in front of you to your left hip — almost like you are wearing a sash and tracing over it with your hand. You can also search for this sign online to see it in action by searching "sign language for Lord."
pondered	Tap your forehead as if you are thinking.
all	Sweep your hands around the room as if gesturing to a large crowd of people.
delight	Hold hands palm up and raise them to about eye level.

Experience

materials needed

- [ ] Small rock or pebble (non-porous so it will sink in water)
- [ ] Container of water to drop the rock into

I'm so excited to learn about light, but before we dive into our study of God's creation and light, we first need to know how we study science.

Do you remember what science is? [Answers may vary, but should be similar to: science is a tool God has given us to learn about and explore the world He created.]

Science is an amazing tool God has given us to learn about and explore the world He created. Science helps us ask important questions, think of ideas, and then share what we learned with our friends and family. Experiments are one way to test our ideas and answer our questions. Do you want to try an experiment? Me too!

Activity directions:

[Teacher grab small rock] I have a question! I wonder if this rock will sink or float in water? What do you think? [Allow student to answer.]

What we think will happen is called our hypothesis. Can you say that word with me? Hypothesis — that is a fun word! A hypothesis is what we think will happen. We can do an experiment to see if what we think will happen — our hypothesis — is what actually does happen.

[Give the student the rock and ask them to place it in the water. Observe what happens.]

Did you think the rock would sink or float in the water before we tried it? [Allow student to answer.]

What happened when we dropped the rock in the water? [Allow student to answer.]

That is so neat. This is how science helps us answer our questions! We asked a question, thought of our hypothesis — what we thought would happen — and tested it with an experiment. Isn't science cool?

· ·

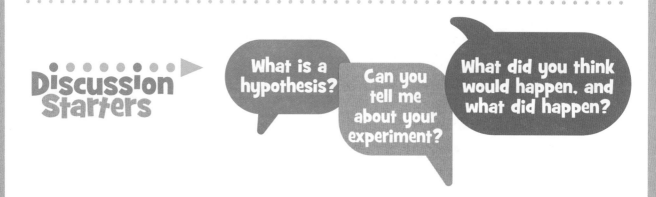

Discussion Starters

What is a hypothesis?

Can you tell me about your experiment?

What did you think would happen, and what did happen?

• Your student may also enjoy guiding a sibling, parent, or grandparent through this simple experiment. Encourage them to teach the word "hypothesis" as they help someone else do this experiment.

• Think of another simple experiment you can do with your student. Develop your hypothesis and test it together!

name

Trace the word hypothesis and draw a picture of people thinking.

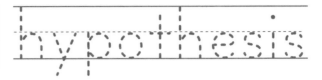

Day

Share

materials needed

- ☐ 3-ring binder for student's Science Notebook
- ☐ Crayons or colored pencils

Teacher tip: If applicable, your student may also create a cover for or decorate their Science Notebook.

Detach sheet and complete. Once completed, student may add the page to their Science Notebook.

We've had so much fun this week learning about science! I have one more surprise for you. As we study science this year, we are also going to create an awesome Science Notebook!

Science helps us share what we learned with our friends and family. Our Science Notebook will help us record what we've learned each week so that we can tell others about it, too!

This week, we learned that science is an amazing tool God has given us to learn about and explore the world He created. We learned that when we do an experiment, what we think will happen is called our hypothesis.

We did an experiment with the rock and the water, and we saw the rock sink in the water. Let's draw a comic strip of our experiment so that we can share what happened with our friends and family!

name

Square I:
Draw a picture of yourself asking a question.

We had a question: Would the rock sink in water?

Square 2:
Draw your hypothesis. Did you think the rock would sink or float in the water?

This is what I thought would happen when we dropped the rock into the water.

Square 3:
Draw what happened when you dropped the rock in the water.

This is what happened!

The First Day of Creation

1st Day of Creation

Day

Learn

This week, we are going to jump right into our study of God's creation. Are you excited? I know I am! I have some questions. I wonder if you do, too? I wonder who made the heavens and the earth? Do you remember what we start with when we study science? [Give student a moment to answer. Answer should be the Bible.]

First, we always start by taking our questions to the Bible! To find the answers to our question, we'll start in the first book of the Bible, Genesis. Here's what the Bible says there:

In the beginning God created the heavens and the earth. Now the earth was formless and empty, darkness was over the surface of the deep, and the Spirit of God was hovering over the waters" (Genesis 1:1–2).

I think I heard the answer to our question. Did you hear it, too? Who made the heavens and the earth? [God.]

Wow! At the very beginning, God created the heavens and the earth. God created the earth, and it was covered in water — no dry land yet! The earth wasn't done yet because God would continue creating.

We also heard that the earth was covered in darkness. I wonder who

flashlight ✓

Weekly materials list

27

created light and when light was made? Where do you think we should look for the answer? In the Bible! Let's keep reading:

And God said, "Let there be light," and there was light. God saw that the light was good, and he separated the light from the darkness. God called the light "day," and the darkness he called "night." And there was evening and there was morning — the first day (Genesis 1:3-5).

I think we may have found our answers in those verses! Can you answer our questions from what we just read in the Bible?

Who made light? [God.]

When was light made? [The first day of creation.]

And one more question: What did God call the light? [Day.]

God made the heavens, earth, and light on the very first day of creation. How amazing! We are going to learn more about the heavens and earth as we continue our study of creation, but first, we'll talk more about light in our next few lessons.

For today, let's have some fun! God created the heavens, earth, and light on the first day of creation. Do you remember what He called the light and darkness? God called the light "day" and he called the darkness "night."

name

Trace then copy the word day and draw a picture of daytime.

Trace then copy the word night and draw a picture of nighttime.

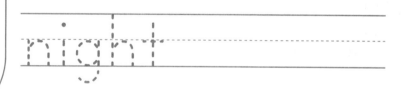

Discussion Starters

Who made the heavens, earth, and light?

When were they made?

What did God call light?

What is your favorite part of the day?

What is your favorite part of the night?

Day

Experience

materials needed

☐ Flashlight

Today, we're going to play with light! Light is energy that travels. Let's go into a dark room and see how light travels!

We are going to turn off the light in the room, and then I will turn on the flashlight. We'll be able to see the light travel to the other side of the room. Do you think the light will travel quickly or slowly? [Allow student to answer.]

You think the light will travel _____ .
[fill in with student's answer]

This is what you think will happen. Do you remember what that is called?
[Allow student to answer.]

This is called your hypothesis — what you think will happen! Your hypothesis is that the light will travel _____ .
[fill in with student's answer]

Now let's see what happens!

Activity directions:

Take a flashlight into a dark room.
Turn it on and observe
the beam instantly travel to the
opposite side of the room.

What did you see?

Did the light travel quickly or slowly?

When we turned on the flashlight, did the light travel quickly or slowly to the other side of the room? Is that what you thought would happen?

When we turned on the light in the room, did it take a long time to light up or was it bright in the room right away?

In our experiment, we saw that light traveled very fast to the other side of the room! In fact, light moves so quickly, it traveled to the other side of the room instantly!

Through many experiments scientists have done, we know that light travels very quickly. Light travels at 186,000 miles per second in a vacuum — that means when there is no matter or material to block it. When we drive in a car, we can travel about 50–60 miles per hour, but light can travel at 186,000 miles per second. That is so much faster than I can even imagine. God made light pretty amazing!

There is so much more we are going to learn about light as we continue our science adventure through creation!

Discussion Starters

Does light travel quickly or slowly?

What was your hypothesis?

Was it right or wrong?

- Your student may also enjoy guiding a family member through this experiment and teaching them that light travels quickly.

- Allow the student to play with the flashlight as they watch light travel.

Share

name

This week, we learned that light travels super fast! We want to share what we've learned about light with others, so now it's time to add a page to our Science Notebook! Let's color the picture and copy the words "Light travels fast" on the back of this page.

Light travels fast.

Tear out for Science Notebook

Trace then copy the words "Light travels fast."

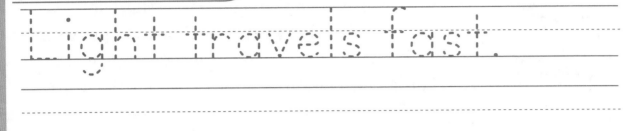

Draw a picture of your flashlight.

Light Is Made of Colors

1st Day of Creation

Day

Learn

Are you ready to learn even more about light? I'm so excited. Let's get started! Through studying God's creation, we know that light has certain properties. Properties is a word that means a quality or trait. But what does that mean? Hmm, what color are your eyes? [Allow student to answer.]

Your eye color is one of your traits or properties — it is a part of you. Maybe you are a very hard worker, you are honest, or take really good care of things — these would also be traits, or properties, of you.

Light also has certain traits, or properties, about it. I wonder if Adam and Eve ever talked with God about the properties of light? We can imagine that one day, maybe Adam told Cain and Abel about the properties of light. . . .

White sheet of paper	✓
Glass prism	☐
Light source	☐

Weekly materials list

Imagine That!
Bible-inspired stories

The sun was up — it was day! Abel jumped up from his bed. "Where are you going so fast?" asked Cain.

"Dad is going to teach me about light today! I am so excited to learn about God's creation. Come with me!" said Abel. Cain got up, and they both ran to Adam and Eve.

"Dad, Dad, Dad, can we start?" Abel exclaimed.

"Yes, tell us about light!" Cain chimed in.

Eve laughed, "Calm down, boys! Give your Dad a minute to finish eating. Here, sit. Eat some breakfast, and we will talk about light."

Adam chuckled. "Well, boys, God made light. Light is energy, and it travels very fast. The light we see is made of many colors: red, orange, yellow, green, blue, indigo, and violet. We can't usually see all of those colors in the light, but they are there."

Adam thought quietly for a minute. "The colors in light are like God. We can't always see them, but we know they are there. We can't see God either, but we know that He is also always there."

Abel thought about what his dad had said as he finished eating breakfast. "Thank you, God, that you are always there, even though we can't see you," he prayed as he got up to play.

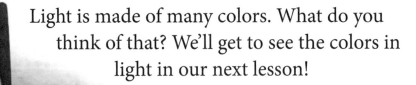

Light is made of many colors. What do you think of that? We'll get to see the colors in light in our next lesson!

name

Teacher tip: Think of a character trait your student has and point it out to them as they complete the worksheet.

Light has certain properties, and so do you! Do you work hard or take good care of people, pets, or things? Are you honest or can you make people laugh at a silly joke? Draw a picture of you!

Discussion Starters ► Can you explain what a property or trait is?

Discuss character traits with your student. What are some good character traits they have? What are some they can model from a friend or family member?

Experience

materials needed

- White sheet of paper
- Glass prism (acrylic will also work)
- Light source — natural light outside or through a window is best, but a flashlight will also work.

We learned in our last lesson that light is made of many colors. Would you like to see those colors? Me too! Today, we'll get to do an experiment. Let's get started!

Activity directions:

If a natural light source is available:

1. Stand outside or in front of a window. Have student hold the white piece of paper under the prism.

2. Hold prism lengthwise. Rotate until the rainbow colors appear on the sheet of paper. If no rainbow becomes visible, adjust the angle the prism is held at and continue rotating until the rainbow appears. Observe the colors. Your student may also draw what they see.

If a natural light source is not available:

1. Take a flashlight and the prism into a dark room. Stand anywhere in the room.

2. Hold the prism in one hand and shine the flashlight toward the prism with the other hand. Look around the room to find the rainbow. If the rainbow is not immediately visible, adjust the angle of the prism and/or how close the flashlight is to the prism until the rainbow becomes visible on a wall. Observe the colors. Your student may also draw what they see.

Wow! That was really neat. Light is made of many colors! When the sun comes up or we turn on a light, those colors are there, but we don't usually see them. We call this "white light." The prism bends the white light that comes through it and splits all the colors apart so that we can see them separately. It's pretty neat, isn't it?

What does the prism do to light?

Allow your student to use the prism (under direct supervision if they are using a glass prism). Can they make a rainbow outside or in another window?

Did you know the Bible also compares God to light? In John 8:12, Jesus said ... *"I am the light of the world. Whoever follows me will never walk in darkness, but will have the light of life."*

Psalm 119:105 says, *"Your word is a lamp for my feet, a light on my path."*

When we see light — whether when the sun comes up or we turn on a light — we know that light is made of many colors. Even though we can't see those colors without the help of a prism, we know they are there! And we know that God is always there too, even though we can't see Him. We learn some pretty amazing lessons from science, don't we?

 **Let's memorize**

Psalm 119:105

" **Your word** is a **lamp** for my feet, a light on my **path**. "

	Actions
Your	Point your fingers, as if pointing to someone.
word	Place hands together, palm to palm. Open hands, as if opening a book.
lamp	Pretend to hold a lantern over your head.
path	Walk in place.

Share

We've asked many questions about light over the last few weeks. Questions like, who made light, and when was it made? We learned that God created light on the first day of creation. We also learned that light travels fast at 186,000 miles per second and it is made of many colors.

Science helps us share what we learn about God's world with others—we can tell someone else that light is made of many colors. Let's add a page to our Science Notebook today!

name

A prism helps us see the colors in light! Color in the prism rainbow below and show it to a friend or family member. You can tell them what we learned this week about light — and that light reminds us of God!

Light Waves

1st Day of Creation

Learn

Last week, we learned that the light we see is made of colors, and we used a prism to help us see those colors. It was pretty neat, wasn't it? Do you remember the colors we saw? [Allow student to answer.]

We saw red, orange, yellow, green, blue, indigo, and violet! Light is energy that travels very quickly, and it is made of many colors. God's creation is amazing, isn't it?

We'll learn more about light today! Light is made of colors, and each of those colors travels in a wave pattern. We call this a wavelength. I wonder if Adam and Eve ever asked God how the colors in light travel? Put on your imagination cap, and let's imagine what they may have told their children! In our last story, Cain and Abel had learned about light. Let's imagine what happened later that day.

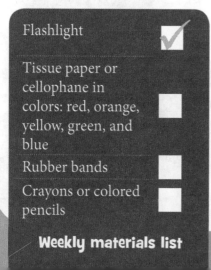

Flashlight	✓
Tissue paper or cellophane in colors: red, orange, yellow, green, and blue	☐
Rubber bands	☐
Crayons or colored pencils	☐

Weekly materials list

Imagine That!
Bible-inspired stories

It was now the end of the day. Adam, Cain, and Abel had worked hard taking care of the earth. Cain had stepped on a thorn that day — ouch! Eve pulled the thorn from his foot with care and washed it with cool water until the stinging stopped.

"I'm sorry, Cain," Eve said softly. "There didn't use to be thorns. They came after our sin. Sin hurts us in many ways."

That evening, they ate dinner together and talked as the sun set. "It was fun to learn about light today, Dad!" said Cain.

"It sure was!" Abel exclaimed. "Is there anything else you can tell us about light?" Abel asked.

Adam thought for a minute. He thought back to the Garden of Eden. "Hmm, yes, yes, there is! I asked God many questions about His creation. I learned that light is made of colors, and each color — red, orange, yellow, green, blue, indigo, and violet — travels in waves."

Adam knelt down to the ground and used his finger to draw wave patterns in the dirt. "Red travels in a loose wave, just like this. Blue travels in a tighter wave — like this," he said as he illustrated the wavelengths.

"God's creation is so amazing, boys, there are incredible things that we can see and many more incredible things we cannot see."

The colors we see travel in waves. Can you use your finger to trace the wavelengths?

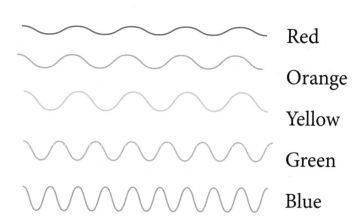

Visible Light

Red

Orange

Yellow

Green

Blue

Do you remember what we call these waves? [Allow student to answer.]

We call them wavelengths! As light travels, objects around us either absorb or reflect the colors in light. That means when you see a big red apple, it's because the apple is reflecting the red wavelength back to your eyes. Or, when you see a yellow banana, the banana is reflecting the yellow wavelength back to your eyes. How cool is that? We'll learn a bit more about wavelengths as we continue talking about light, and I can hardly wait!

Discussion Starters

Do the colors in light travel in a straight line or in a wave pattern?

What do we call the wave pattern?

What is your favorite thing about light?

name

Let's practice writing these words!

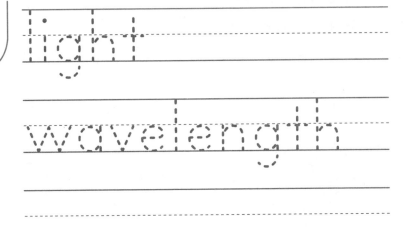

light

wavelength

Color the fruit with the right color.

red

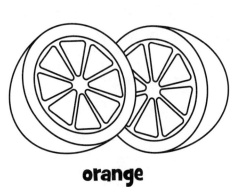

orange

yellow

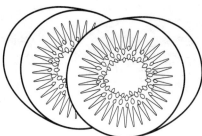

green

blue

Day

Experience

materials needed

- ☐ Flashlight

- ☐ Tissue paper or cellophane in colors: red, orange, yellow, green, blue

- ☐ Rubber bands (Optional, to hold tissue paper/ cellophane in place on the flashlight. You can also simply use your hand.)

- ☐ Crayons, markers, or colored pencils

This week, we're learning about light waves! The light we see is made of colors, and each color travels in a wave pattern called a wavelength. Today, we are going to play with light colors and draw the wavelength for each color!

Activity directions:

Choose one color of tissue paper or cellophane and wrap the flashlight beam up in that color — the light won't travel far but it should cast the hue of the color wrapped around it onto the worksheet. If the color is not readily visible, wrap a second layer of the same color around the light.

Shine the flashlight at the start of each color's wavelength on the worksheet. Have the student trace the wavelength of that color with the corresponding crayon color.

name

Trace the wavelength with the right color.

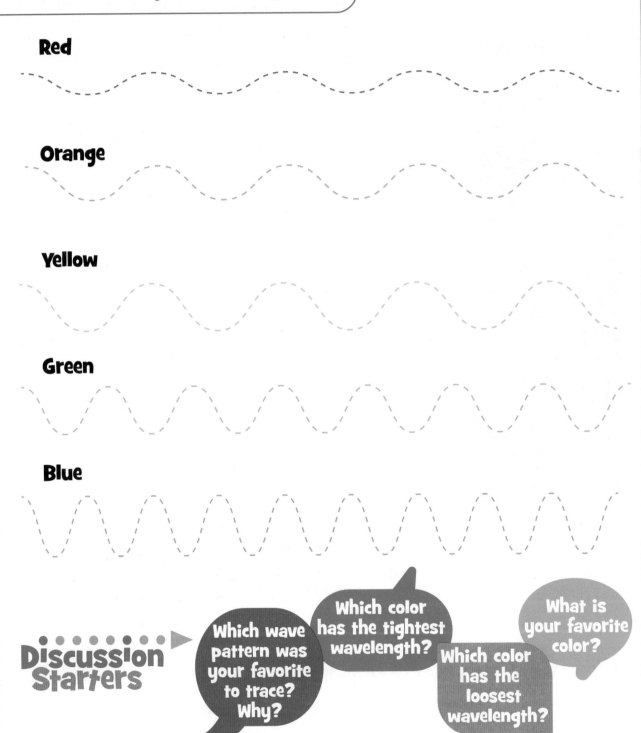

Red

Orange

Yellow

Green

Blue

Discussion Starters

Which wave pattern was your favorite to trace? Why?

Which color has the tightest wavelength?

Which color has the loosest wavelength?

What is your favorite color?

Go on a color treasure hunt! See if your student can find objects that are red, yellow, green, and blue. Add any other colors to the hunt.

48

Day

Share

name

This week, we learned that each color in light travels in a wavelength! Do you know what this means? We get to add another page to our Science Notebook today — yay! Let's finish the wavelengths for each color and add this page to your Science Notebook. Then, show your page to a friend or family member as you tell them what you learned this week about God's Creation: light travels in waves!

Finish the wavelength for each color.

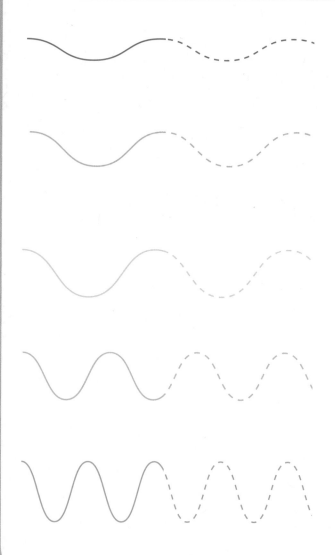

Trace the letters.

Light travels
in waves!

Do you remember Psalm 119:105? Let's say it!
Color the big words.

"Your word

is a lamp for my feet,

a light on my path."

Rainbows

1st Day of Creation

Day **Learn**

We are almost done with our study of light. We've been learning so much and have had a lot of fun! This week, we get to learn about something very special light can do. Do you remember when we used the prism to help us see the colors in light? Did you know that water can also be a prism? It's true!

Water droplets can bend light just like a prism so that we can see the colors in light. Do you know what it is called when this happens? [Allow student to answer.] A rainbow! Hmm, I have a few questions about rainbows. I wonder who made the rainbow — and what does it mean? Do you wonder, too? Where do you think we should take our questions? [Allow student to answer.]

The Bible! For the answers to our questions, we're going to travel further into the Book of Genesis in the Bible — to the days of Noah. Do you remember Noah? [Allow student to answer.]

God told Noah to build an Ark because He would be sending a flood to the earth. You can read more of Noah's story in the Bible in Genesis chapters 6–9. After the Flood, Noah and his family left the ark and worshipped God. They made an offering there to worship God. Let's read from the Bible and see if we can answer our questions about rainbows — who made the rainbow and what does it mean?

And God said, "This is the sign of the covenant I am making between me and you and every living creature with you, a covenant for all generations to come: I have set my rainbow in the clouds, and it will be the sign of the covenant between me and the earth. Whenever I bring clouds over the earth and the rainbow appears in the clouds, I will remember my covenant between me and you and all living creatures of every kind. Never again will the waters become a flood to destroy all life. Whenever the rainbow appears in the clouds, I will see it and remember the everlasting covenant between God and all living creatures of every kind on the earth" (Genesis 9:12–16).

"Covenant" is a big word that means an agreement or a promise. God made the rainbow, and it is His promise to us that He will never flood the whole earth again. I think we found the answers to our questions!

Who made the rainbow? [God.]

What does the rainbow mean? [Answer may be similar to the rainbow is God's promise that He will never flood the whole earth again.]

I'm ready for some fun! How about you?

Option A:	
Garden hose with nozzle that allows mist	✔
Sunny day	☐
Water source for hose	☐
Optional: Paper, crayons, and surface to draw on	☐
Option B:	
Smooth glass cup, filled with water	☐
White sheet of paper	☐
Flashlight	☐
DVD or CD	☐

Weekly materials list

Discussion Starters ● ● ● ● ● ● ● ● ► What does the rainbow mean?

- Read Noah's story in Genesis 6–9.

- Read *When You See a Rainbow*, available from Master Books.

name

Color the picture of Noah and the rainbow!

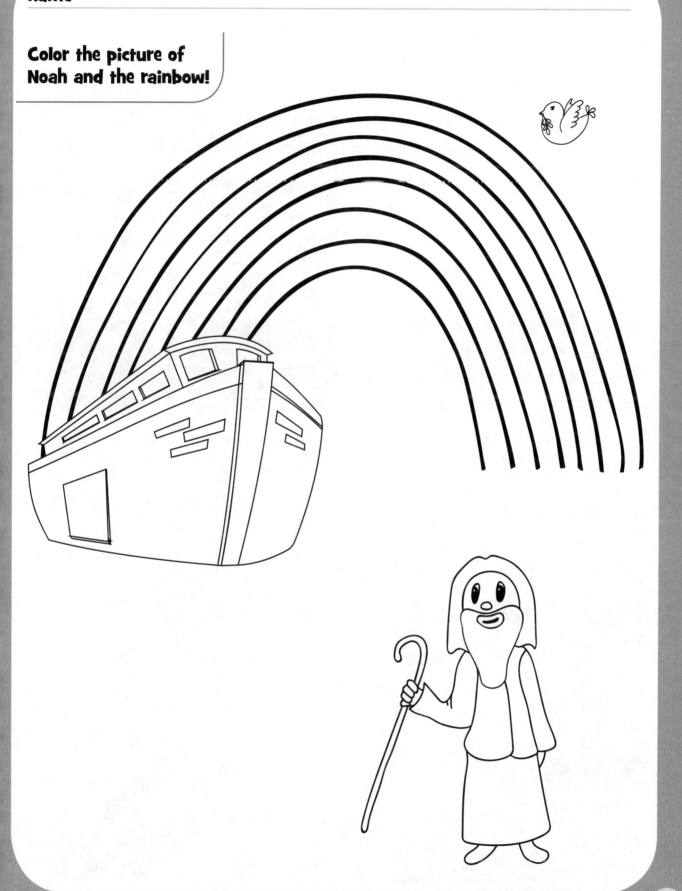

Experience

We're learning about rainbows this week! Do you remember what the rainbow is? [Allow student to answer. Answer may be similar to the rainbow is God's promise that He will never flood the whole earth again.]

Today we are going to make a rainbow! Water acts like a prism. It can also bend white light so that we see the colors in the rainbow. Are you ready? Let's get started!

materials needed

Option A (recommended) — Outdoor Rainbow

☐ Garden hose with nozzle that allows mist

☐ Water source for hose

☐ Sunny day

Optional: Paper, crayons, and surface to draw

materials needed

Option B— Indoor Rainbow

☐ Drinking glass, smooth glass is the best

☐ Water

☐ White sheet of paper

☐ Flashlight

☐ DVD or CD

Activity directions:

Option A-outdoor rainbow	Option B-Indoor rainbow

Option A-outdoor rainbow

1. Go outside with your student and locate an area where the sun is shining brightly. Bring the garden hose over and turn on the water supply.

2. Ask your student to stand with their back to the sun in between the sun and the hose. Stand off to the side of the student, 5–10 feet in front of them, and begin to spray the water on a mist/fine droplet setting. A rainbow should become visible to the student in the mist. If it is not immediately visible, have them move and rotate around the water's path until the rainbow becomes visible.

Optional: Have student use paper and crayons to draw what they see as you continue to spray water.

Option B-Indoor rainbow

1. Fill the drinking glass with water, leaving 1–2 inches of space from the top of the glass. Place the glass on a white sheet of paper. Hold the flashlight at a slight angle about 3–5 inches away from the glass. The water line in the glass should be about level with the halfway point of the flashlight lens.

2. Adjust the flashlight angle and distance until the colors become visible on the paper. (Note: the colors will be bent or create a pattern on the paper rather than a full rainbow shape.) You may also dim the room lights to make the rainbow more apparent. Point out that water bends light just like a prism, and this creates a rainbow when the sun is out and there are water droplets in the sky.

3. Now, take the DVD or CD and turn it upside down. Hold it about 3–5 inches away from a wall and shine the flashlight toward it. The disc should reflect a full rainbow onto the wall — like a rainbow we see in the sky. Adjust the angle or distance of the disc and/or light if it is not readily visible.

Optional: Your student may draw what they see.

Discussion Starters

What is your favorite color in the rainbow?

How does water help to make a rainbow?

Let's memorize

Genesis 9:17 (NIrV)

" So God **said** to Noah, 'The rainbow is the sign of my covenant. I have made my covenant between **me** and **all** life on earth.' "

	Actions
said	Touch your hand to your mouth and move it away.
rainbow	Place both hands above your head and spread them apart, tracing the shape of the rainbow in the sky.
me	Point to the sky.
all	Sweep your hands around the room as if gesturing to a large crowd of people.

The rainbow is so amazing, and it is an important reminder of a very special promise from God. Do you remember what that promise is? [Allow student to answer. Answer may be similar to the rainbow is God's promise that He will never flood the whole earth again.]

Today is the day we get to share what we've learned and add another cool page to our Science Notebook!

This is a picture of a rainbow in the sky. Can you draw this picture on the back of this page? Or draw a picture of a rainbow you've seen in the sky? Then, add this page to your Science Notebook and share what you've learned! The rainbow is a reminder to us of God's special promise to never flood the whole earth again.

name

Draw a rainbow. You can turn the page sideways if you need more room!

The Second Day of Creation

2nd Day of Creation

Day Learn

We've learned so much about light in our last few lessons. We learned that God created light, that light travels fast, that light is made of many colors, the colors travel in waves, and we even learned about the rainbow! God's creation is so amazing, and there is so much more we can explore!

Do you remember what day of creation God made light on? [Answer should be the first day.] God made light and darkness on the first day of creation. Are you ready to explore the second day of creation? Me too! I wonder what God made on the second day . . . where do you think we should take our question? [Allow student to answer.]

The Bible! Let's read from the first book of the Bible, Genesis: *God said, "Let there be a huge space between the waters. Let it separate water from water." And that's exactly what happened. God made the huge space between the waters. He separated the water under the space from the water above it. God called the huge space "sky." There was evening, and there was morning. It was day two (Genesis 1:6–8; NIrV).*

I think I heard our answer. Did you hear it, too?

What did God make on the second day? [The sky.]

Do you think Adam and Eve asked God questions about the sky? Let's imagine what they may have learned as we continue our story!

Crayons ✓

Weekly materials list

Imagine That!
Bible-inspired stories

The next day, the boys were up early. They helped their mom, Eve, gather and make some breakfast.

Abel spoke quietly as he picked some grapes. "Mom, we have learned all about the first day of creation and so many neat things about light. What did God make next? Did you ask Him about it?"

"Oh, yes! As you learned, God made the heavens, earth, and light on the first day of creation. On the second day of creation, God made the sky," Eve replied as she motioned to the clear blue sky.

"The sky is so, so . . . big!" Cain exclaimed.

"It sure is, Cain," Eve replied as she looked to the sky. "The sky is vast — that is a word that means very large. The vastness of the sky reminds us that God is great."

Abel looked up to the sky. It was so clear and blue. "Mom," he asked, puzzled. "Why is the sky blue?"

"I wondered that too, buddy, so one evening, I asked God!" Eve thought back to the Garden of Eden and her conversation with God as they had walked and talked that night.

"Remember the colors in light Dad taught you?"

"Mhm!" both boys answered.

Eve continued, "Well, the light from the sun is white light made of all those colors. As the sunlight shines through the sky, the atmosphere scatters the blue light all over the place! When we look at the sky, our eyes see the color blue bouncing around and being reflected into our eyes."

Cain looked back up to the sky. "Wow!"

"Let's go eat now. We have a lot to do today, boys!" Eve said as they walked back toward their tent.

. . . .

We are going to study the sky for our next few lessons, and it's going to be amazing!

Discussion Starters

Go for a walk and observe the sky.

Are there clouds?

Do you see any interesting objects?

What did God make on the second day of creation?

name

Circle the things you may see in the sky!

Today, we are going to observe the sky. Let's get ready to go outside!

Activity directions:

materials needed

☐ Crayons

Experience

I'm going to ask some questions as we look at the sky outside. You can circle what you see!

Is the sky clear or cloudy today?

Is the sun out, or hidden by clouds?

Can you see a lot of the sky or just a small area?

What color is the sky?

Color the box to show the color you see!

Did you notice anything interesting in the sky? Have your teacher write your answer here:

_____

_____

Discussion Starters

Describe what you noticed in the sky today.

Let your student take a friend or family member outside to see what they can observe together.

Airplanes fly high in the sky! Can you finish the picture by connecting the dots?

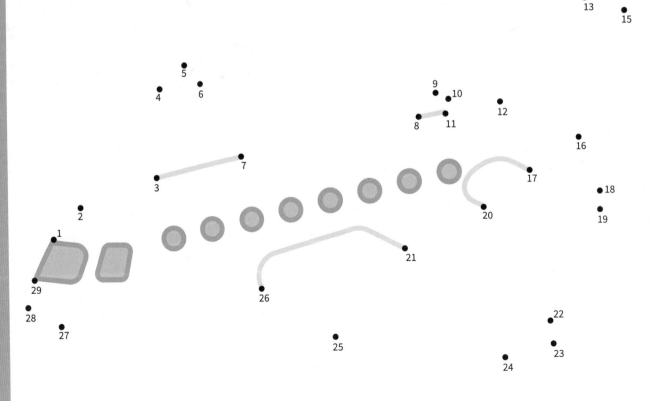

name _____

Share

Yesterday, we observed the sky. Today, we want to share what we saw! We can use our notes from yesterday to remind us what we saw. Then, draw a picture of the sky below and trace the words "God made the sky." Then, add this page to your Science Notebook.

Draw a sky picture!

Trace and copy the words below.

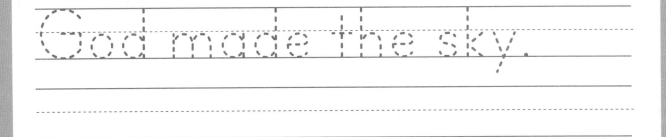

Atmosphere

2nd Day of Creation

Day Learn

God made the sky on the second day of creation. When we look at the sky, it looks big and blue. Maybe we see birds flying, clouds, and even an airplane way up high!

Did you know there is more to the sky than what we see with our bare eyes? It's true! Scientists study the sky, and they've organized it into five amazing layers. The layers God created in the sky help protect the earth, keep us safe, and make the earth a great place to live. When we study the sky, we see God's care for us and His mercy. Let's learn about the layers of the sky!

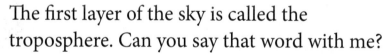

The first layer of the sky is called the troposphere. Can you say that word with me? Troposphere. The troposphere is the first layer of the sky, and it's about 11 miles high in most places. We see clouds, birds, and airplanes in the troposphere!

The second layer of the sky is called the stratosphere. Can you say that word with me? Stratosphere. The stratosphere is around 30 miles high above the troposphere. It is the second layer of the sky. God put something very special in this layer of the sky — the ozone layer!

Glue stick ✓

Crayons, colored pencils, or markers ☐

Scissors ☐

Weekly materials list

Ozone is a special gas, and it helps filter out the harmful rays of the sun called ultraviolet, or UV rays for short. We see God's care and protection of us in the ozone layer of the stratosphere!

The third layer of the sky is called the mesosphere. Can you say that word with me? Mesosphere. The mesosphere is about 53 miles high above the stratosphere. It is the third layer of the sky. Have you ever seen a shooting star in the sky? If you have seen a shooting star, what you saw was a meteor burning up in the mesosphere as it traveled.

Wow! So far, we've learned the first three layers of the sky, and each is very specially designed. In our next lesson, we'll learn the next two layers of the sky!

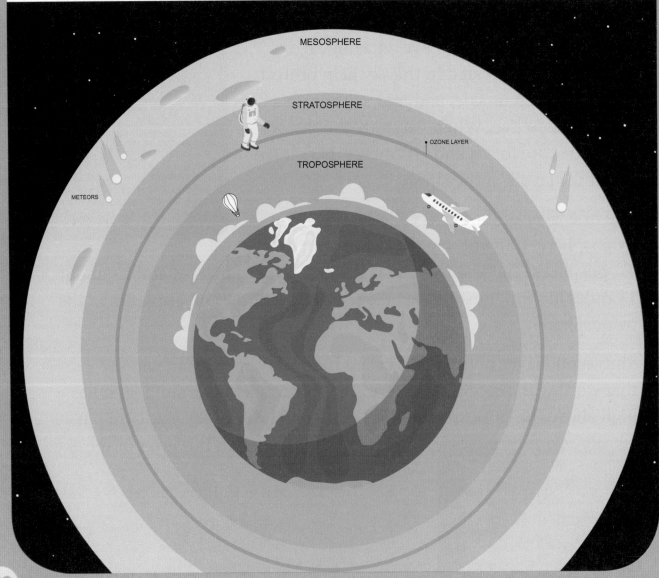

name

Color the first layer of the sky.

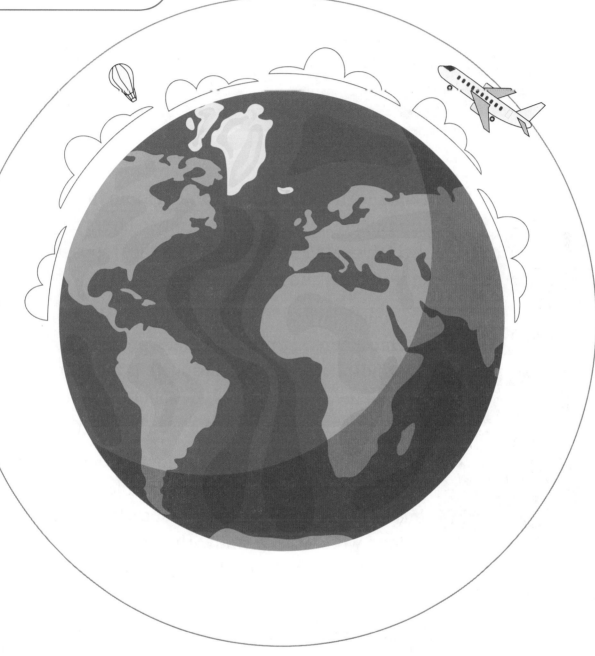

What is the first layer of the sky?

What might we see in that layer?

What is the second layer of the sky?

What is the special gas in this layer?

Day

Experience

materials needed

☐ Glue stick

☐ Crayons, colored pencils, or markers

☐ Scissors

Today, we'll travel much higher up into the atmosphere as we learn the last two layers of the sky! We've already learned about the troposphere, stratosphere, and mesosphere.

The fourth layer of the atmosphere is called the thermosphere. Can you say that word with me? Thermosphere. The thermosphere is the fourth layer of the sky. This layer goes about 350 miles high above the mesosphere. It is a very big layer!

Have you heard of the International Space Station? The International Space Station is called a spacecraft. It is like a big house in space that astronauts can live in for a while as they study. The International Space Station orbits the earth in the thermosphere! You may also find other satellites in this layer.

The fifth layer of the atmosphere is called the exosphere. Can you say that word with me? Exosphere. The exosphere is the fifth layer of the sky. This layer is around 40,000 miles high above the thermosphere — much, much bigger than the thermosphere. You may find more satellites orbiting the earth in this layer. At the very far edge of the exosphere is outer space.

Whew, we've traveled so high up in the atmosphere. I'm ready for some fun! How about you? Let's put together the layers of the sky! Cut out each layer of the sky from this page and glue it above the earth on the next page.

EXOSPHERE

THERMOSPHERE

MESOSPHERE

STRATOSPHERE

TROPOSPHERE

SATELLITES

SPACECRAFT

OZONE LAYER
20 - 30 km

AIRPLANE

INTERNATIONAL SPACE STATION

METEORS

Blank for cutting out atmosphere.

name

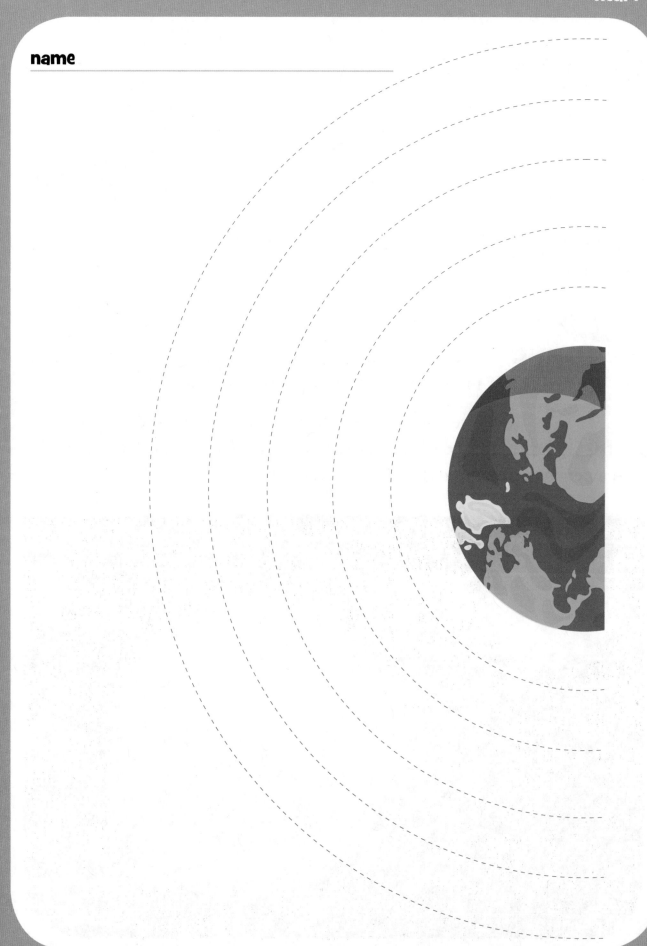

Discussion Starters

- Pick one layer of the sky and explore it deeper at the library or through NASA. Be sure to preview any material first.

- Search for a video tour online of the International Space Station. Talk about what it might be like to live there for a month!

What is the third layer of the sky?

Do you remember what a meteor does in this layer of the sky?

Day :::

SHARE

We learned so much about the atmosphere this week, and it was really neat! God made the sky and all the layers of the atmosphere. Do you remember the names of those layers? They are the troposphere, stratosphere, mesosphere, thermosphere, and exosphere!

The atmosphere helps keep earth safe, and it reminds us that God cares for us. We want to share what we've learned. Today, we'll add a new page to our your Science Notebook.

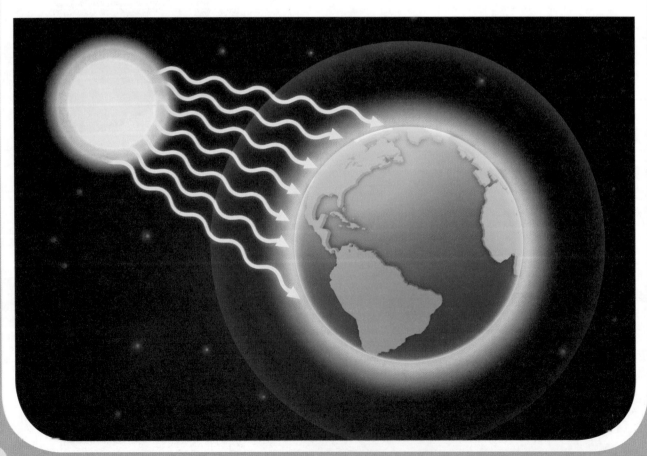

name

Color the layers of the earth's atmosphere.

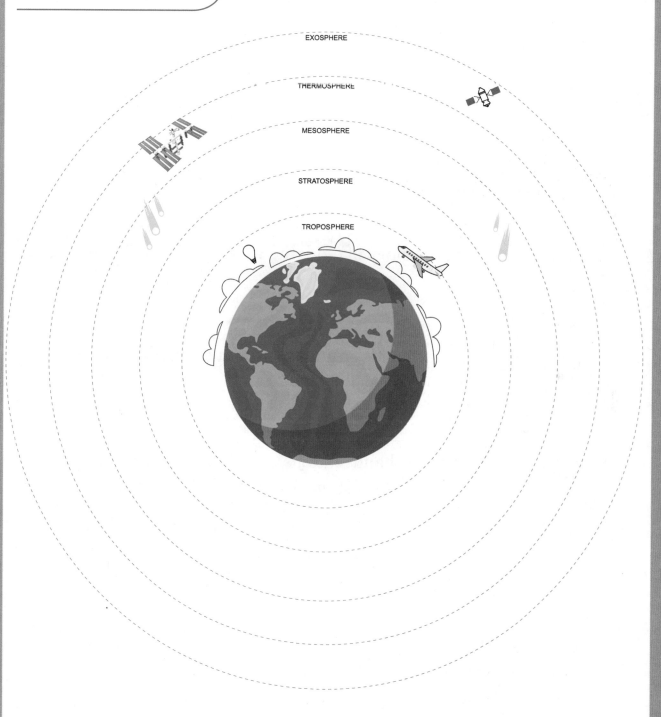

EXOSPHERE

THERMOSPHERE

MESOSPHERE

STRATOSPHERE

TROPOSPHERE

God made the atmosphere!

Trace the words "God made the atmosphere!"

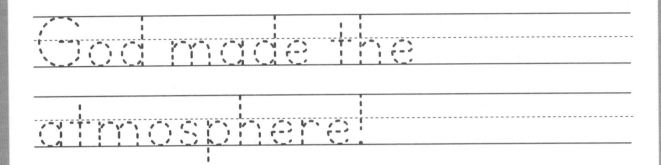

 **Let's memorize**

Psalm 19:1

"The heavens **declare** the glory of God; the **skies** proclaim the **work** of his **hands.**"

	Actions
declare	Put your hands around your mouth, like you're shouting something.
skies	Point up to the sky.
work	Make your hands into fists, with the palms facing down. Tap one fist on the top of the other hand.
hands	Put your hands up and shake them.

Condensation and Evaporation

2nd Day of Creation

Day

Learn Let's talk about condensation and evaporation today! Those are two really big words, aren't they? Can you say them with me? Condensation and evaporation. They are important words to know as we continue to study the sky, because we are going to study clouds and rain next. Clouds and rain both depend on condensation and evaporation.

So, what is evaporation? Well, evaporation is the process of a liquid — like water — becoming a gas in the air. Have you ever watched steam rise from a pot of water as it begins to boil on the stove? Or have you seen the steam float through the air in the bathroom when you take a shower or bath? This is evaporation happening!

Were you listening closely? Can you tell me what evaporation is? [Allow student to answer. Answer should be similar to evaporation is water becoming gas in the air.]

When water evaporates, it becomes gas in the air and travels in very, very tiny droplets of water. We call this water vapor. As the water vapor travels through the air, it will eventually begin to cool and turn back into a liquid — water! When the water vapor cools and turns back into a liquid, we call this condensation.

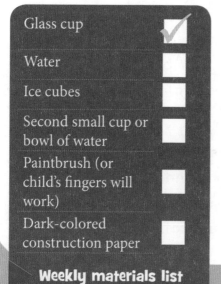

Glass cup	✓
Water	☐
Ice cubes	☐
Second small cup or bowl of water	☐
Paintbrush (or child's fingers will work)	☐
Dark-colored construction paper	☐

Weekly materials list

77

Condensation is water vapor becoming a liquid again as it cools.

There was our big word again! Can you tell me what condensation is?

[Allow student to answer. Answer should be similar to condensation is water vapor becoming a liquid again as it cools.]

I wonder if Adam and Eve ever noticed condensation and evaporation? Maybe they asked God about it and taught their sons one day. Let's imagine!

· ·

Imagine That
Bible-inspired stories

It was after lunch time, and Cain and Abel were playing in the field, not far from their tent. Eve stepped outside and called to them, "Cain, Abel, I need your help. Please help me fill the jars with water from the stream."

"Yes, Mom!" they called as they ran to her.

Cain and Abel picked up a clay jar Eve had made for carrying water easily. In the tent was a larger clay jar that held a few gallons of water for cooking and cleaning during the day.

Eve, Cain, and Abel walked to the stream and filled their jars. Then, they carried them back to the tent and poured the cool water into the big jar. "It is halfway full, boys. Let's make one more trip to the stream to fill it all the way up," Eve said.

They filled their jars once more and walked back to the tent. As they poured the water from the small jars into the big jar, Abel noticed something strange. "Mom, why are there small beads of water on the outside of the jar? We didn't spill any water on it!"

"Ah, that is a very special part of God's creation, son." Eve motioned to the fire pit outside the tent. There were hot coals there, and she was warming water in another container on the coals. "Do you see the steam rising from the water as the coals heat it up? That is evaporation. The water has become a gas and travels in the air. It is water vapor," she said. "It is easy to see the water evaporate as steam, but water evaporates from the stream, too! Anywhere there is water, it is also slowly evaporating."

"Water vapor travels through the air, and as it cools, it can also turn back into water! When we poured the cool stream water into our big jar, the jar became colder than the air. Water vapor from the air then cooled around the jar and turned back in to water, forming those small drops of water on the jar. This is called condensation."

Abel touched the outside of the big jar and his hand became wet. "Wow, God's creation is really amazing, Mom!"

Eve smiled. "Yes, it is, buddy. Yes, it is."

· ·

You and I will get to see condensation and evaporation in our next lesson, too. I'm excited! How about you?

Discussion Starters

Put a pot of water on the stove to boil and watch the steam rise.

What is condensation?

What is evaporation?

Day ²

Experience

materials needed

- [ ] Glass cup
- [ ] Water
- [ ] Ice cubes
- [ ] Second small cup or bowl of water
- [ ] Paintbrush (or child's fingers will work)
- [ ] Dark-colored construction paper

Today, we're going to see evaporation and condensation in action. Are you ready? Let's roll up our sleeves and get started!

First, we are going to put some ice and water in this glass. The water and ice inside the glass will make it cold. Do you think water vapor from the air will condense on the outside of the glass? [Allow the student to answer.]

That is what you think will happen! Do you remember what that is called? This is your hypothesis — what you think will happen!

Well, let's fill our glass with ice and water and wait to see what happens!

While we wait, we will start our second experiment. We are going to use water to paint a picture on a piece of paper. The water will then evaporate from our picture. Do you think the water will evaporate quickly or slowly from the page?

So, you think the water will evaporate ————————————————————— .
[fill in with student's answer]

This is your hypothesis, what you think will happen. Let's paint a water picture on our page and see what does happen!

Teacher tip: direct student to paint the page but monitor so that the page does not become soaked.

I like your picture. Let's check on our glass! Do you see beads of water on the outside of the glass? That is condensation. The glass was cold. As water vapor in the air touched the glass, the water vapor cooled down and the vapor turned back into water droplets. Is that what you thought would happen?

Condensation is really neat! What about our picture? Has the water begun to evaporate yet?

Observe picture; if more time is needed check back in another 30–60 minutes.

The water from our picture evaporated back into the air. It was really cool to get to see evaporation and condensation today, wasn't it?

Discussion Starters

What is condensation?

What is evaporation?

How did the beads of water get on the outside of our glass?

What happened to the water on our painting?

You can see condensation happen on a cold water bottle too! Connect the dots to finish the picture.

34 1
33 2
32 3
31 4
30 ------- 5
29 6
28 7
27 8
26 9
25 10
24 11
23 12
22 13
21 20 19 18 17 16 15 14

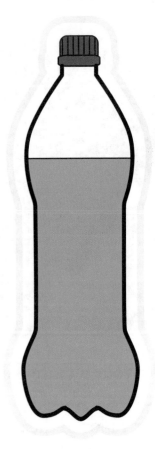

Share

name

Whew! We've learned a lot about condensation and evaporation this week, and I'm so excited to learn how clouds and rain are made of both. Today we want to share what we've learned about God's creation. Let's add a page to our Science Notebook. Don't forget to share what you learned with someone!

Condensation

Evaporation

We can see evaporation and condensation happen when we cook or eat a meal. When we cook food, steam rises from the pan. This is evaporation! When we eat a meal, we may see steam rise from our plate too. You can also see condensation happen on your cup if you have an ice cold glass of water to drink. Can you think of somewhere else you have seen condensation or evaporation in action?

Draw a picture below!

Clouds

2nd Day of Creation

Day

Learn Are you ready for the next part of our exploration of the atmosphere? If we go outside and look up at the sky, what are some things we might see? [Allow student to answer.] We may see birds flying up high, maybe an airplane or helicopter, the sun, and clouds! This week, we are going to study clouds, and we'll even get to make our own cloud. How exciting is that?

Remember when we studied the layers of the atmosphere? We learned about the troposphere, stratosphere, mesosphere, thermosphere, and exosphere. There are a lot of layers in the atmosphere! Clouds are formed in the troposphere and stratosphere, the first and second layers of the atmosphere.

In our last lesson, we learned about evaporation and condensation. As water evaporates and travels high into the sky, it begins to cool and condenses into water droplets or ice crystals. As more and more water vapor condenses, clouds are formed high above us. Clouds are made of tiny droplets of water or ice and dust.

I wonder if Eve taught Cain and Abel about clouds. Let's imagine what they may have talked about. Put on your imagination hat! In our last story, Eve, Cain, and Abel had gathered water and learned about condensation and evaporation. Let's imagine what happened next.

Bible-inspired stories

Abel was tired after going to the stream to fill the big jar with water. He sat on the ground to rest. "Mom, what does water vapor do?" he asked.

"Well, some water vapor becomes clouds. Water vapor is made up of tiny, tiny droplets of water, and it floats in the air, traveling higher and higher in the sky. As it floats higher and higher, it begins to condense — to cool — and that makes clouds high above us. Clouds are filled with water droplets," Eve replied.

Mason jar or tall drinking glass	✓
Lid for mason jar or small saucer to cover glass	
Hot water	
Aerosol spray (hairspray works well)	
2–6 ice cubes	
Elmer's glue®	
Glue stick	
Cotton balls	

Weekly materials list

"Abel, let's run and go tell Dad all about condensation and evaporation! Ready, set, go!" Cain called. Abel quickly got up, and they both ran off to find Adam.

Let's talk about clouds! There are three main types of clouds: cumulus, stratus, and cirrus. Let's learn about each!

Cumulus

Cumulus clouds are fluffy and puffy. They may remind you of cotton balls or even cotton candy in the sky. Sometimes, a cumulus cloud can grow into a thunderstorm. We call that a cumulonimbus cloud, and we'll learn more about that in a few lessons.

Stratus

The next cloud type is stratus clouds. Stratus clouds look like a flat cloud blanket in the sky. They are often grey and gloomy. When you go outside and feel a light misty rain or drizzle, if you look up, you'll likely see stratus clouds blanketing the sky!

The third cloud type is called cirrus. These clouds are very high in the atmosphere. Cirrus clouds look light and feathery because they are made of ice crystals rather than water droplets.

Cirrus

Let's go outside or look out the window. Do you see any clouds in the sky? If there are clouds, let's see if we can identify which type of cloud it is! Are the clouds puffy and fluffy like a cumulus cloud? Or does it look like the sky has a cloud blanket across it like stratus clouds? Are there any light wispy clouds way up high? Then you see cirrus clouds!

name

Let's draw a picture of what we see in the sky, whether it is a clear sunny day, there are a few clouds, or there are lots of clouds in the sky!

Discussion Starters ▶

Can you tell me about cumulus, stratus, or cirrus clouds?

What are clouds made of?

Can you tell me how condensation and evaporation work together to form clouds?

Experience

Today, we're going to make a cloud. Woohoo! Are you ready? Let's get started!

To form, clouds need warm water below them and cold air above and around them. We're going to make a cloud in a jar. Ready?

materials needed

- ☐ Mason jar (recommended) or tall drinking glass

- ☐ Lid for mason jar (recommended) or small saucer to cover glass

- ☐ Hot water (Hot tap will do. If you do not see a cloud form, you may also run water through a coffee maker. Remind young children to be careful and not touch.)

- ☐ Aerosol spray (hairspray works well)

- ☐ 2–6 ice cubes

Activity directions:

Note: In this experiment, the water vapor needs something to cling to in the air within the jar. In the atmosphere, the water droplets cling to dust particles. In our jar, the aerosol spray gives the water droplets something to cling to.

1. Fill mason jar or glass about ½–⅔ of the way full of hot water.

2. With the lid ready, spray the aerosol into the mason jar (1–2 seconds) and cover the jar quickly with the lid.

3. Place ice cubes on top of the lid. (Note: If using a saucer, you may need to move the ice around periodically to ensure it stays over the top of the jar.)

4. Watch inside the jar. You should see a steam cloud forming within a minute or two. (Note: If nothing is visible, remove the lid and see if the cloud rises out of the jar. If not, try again with hotter water and a little more aerosol spray.)

5. Remove the lid and watch the cloud float out of the jar and into the air! Repeat if you'd like.

Did you see the cloud form inside the jar?

Can you describe what you saw?

Wow, that was really neat! Let's talk about what we saw.

Clouds in the sky form in a similar way. Water evaporates from the warm earth below and travels through the sky. As the water vapor travels higher into the sky, it begins to cool and condense in the cold air. Then, it forms a cloud! God's creation is full of amazing things, isn't it?

Discussion Starters

How do clouds form?

What happened inside the jar in our experiment?

Your child may also enjoy doing the cloud experiment with a friend or family member later in the day.

Day

Share

materials needed

☐ Elmer's glue®

☐ Glue stick

☐ Cotton balls

Whew, this week has been so much fun! We studied clouds and even got to create our own cloud. That was my favorite activity! Today, it's time to share what we've learned with others. We're going to add a page to our Science Notebook!

Do you remember the three types of clouds we studied? They are cumulus, stratus, and cirrus clouds. Let's form some clouds on our worksheet with cotton balls, then add this page to our Science Notebook once it's dry!

Cumulus clouds are fluffy and puffy. We can glue cotton balls to our page to form a cumulus cloud. [Note: Elmer's glue® is recommended here.]

Stratus clouds form a cloud blanket. We can pull apart the cotton balls and glue the pieces together to form a cloud blanket. [Note: Elmer's glue® is recommended here.]

Finally, cirrus clouds are feathery. We can pull apart the cotton balls to glue feathery pieces to the page. [Note: Glue stick is recommended here.] **Ready to get started?**

name

Teacher Tip : Help student assemble their cloud worksheet.

cumulus

. . . .

stratus

. . . .

cirrus

Blank for gluing.

The Water Cycle

2nd Day of Creation

Day

Learn

Drip, drop, drip, drop . . . listen with your imagination. Do you hear the rain falling? The rain is falling in our lesson today because we are learning about the water cycle! In our last few lessons, we learned about clouds and how they are formed by evaporation and condensation.

Today, we are going to learn about precipitation. That is what we call it when it rains, hails, sleets, or snows. Evaporation, condensation, and precipitation — those are all really fun words to say! Can you say them with me? Evaporation, condensation, and precipitation.

Water on the earth evaporates — just like we learned last week — and floats through the air as water vapor. Water vapor is made up of many tiny, tiny droplets of water. As the water vapor floats higher into the atmosphere, it begins to condense — to cool — and form clouds. Clouds float high above us, filled with water droplets and ice crystals.

Have you ever carried a gallon of milk or water? It is heavy, isn't it? Clouds are filled with hundreds and hundreds of gallons of water! As more and more water vapor floats to the sky, the tiny water droplets condense and begin to stick together and form clouds. Then, as more

Mason jar or large glass cup of water	✓
Shaving cream	☐
Blue food coloring	☐
Small bowl	☐
Dropper or spoon	☐
Plastic bag or a flat plate (to protect surface)	☐

Weekly materials list

and more water vapor condenses, the droplets of water in the cloud become bigger and heavier.

Clouds are very, very heavy, but they float on the layer of warm air above the earth. God's creation is so amazing! Eventually, the water droplets become too big and heavy for the layer of warm air above the earth to hold them up. When this happens, the water droplets fall out of the cloud and form raindrops. We call this precipitation!

Can you say that word with me? Precipitation! That is what we call it when it rains, hails, sleets, or snows.

Hmm, I wonder if Abel ever asked Adam about rain . . . let's imagine that he did! In our last story, Cain and Abel were running off to find Adam. Let's imagine what happens next.

Imagine That!
Bible-inspired stories

Eve watched the boys as they ran to find Adam. He was tending a field not far from their tent.

"Dad, Dad!" Abel shouted. "Guess what!"

Adam looked up, wiped some sweat from his forehead and smiled. "Hmm, I cannot guess. Tell me, Abel," Adam replied.

"Mom taught us about condensation and evaporation," Abel said breathlessly as Cain interrupted, "And clouds, Dad!"

"Wow, it sounds like you have been learning a lot today! There is something else clouds do. If we wait a bit, I think we may get to learn about that as well." Adam glanced at the sky. It was much cloudier than earlier, and it was starting to look like it may rain.

"Here, help me finish in the field, boys." Adam gave them both a tool, and they began to work. They worked together for awhile, then suddenly, Cain felt a drop of water on the back of his neck. He looked at Abel, who had just felt a drop of water on his hand.

"Um, Dad? Is this what you were talking about?" Cain asked just as it began to slowly rain. Drops of water could be heard as they began to plop on the earth all around them. Drip, drop, drip, drop.

"It sure is!" said Adam. "This is called precipitation — rain!"

They all held out their hands to catch the raindrops. "As water vapor floats higher and condenses in the sky, the water droplets form clouds. The tiny droplets begin to stick together and make bigger and bigger drops of water until the drops are too big and heavy to stay in the cloud anymore. Then, they fall toward the earth and water it. This is one way God cares for His creation," Adam explained.

Suddenly, there were more water drops all around them, and it began to rain hard. The boys looked at each other and said together, "Let's get back to the tent!" And with that, they were off! They ran toward the tent as Adam followed behind.

Adam thought as he walked, "Thank you, God, that you still care for us and the earth. Even though our sin broke the world."

Did you know the Bible talks about God sending rain? In Job 5:9–10 (NIrV), we read this about God: *"He does wonderful things that can't be understood. He does miracles that can't even be counted. He sends rain on the earth. He sends water on the countryside."*

In Psalm 147:7–8 (NIrV), we read, *"Sing to the LORD and give him grateful praise. Make music to our God on the harp. He covers the sky with clouds. He supplies the earth with rain. He makes grass grow on the hills."*

Isn't God's care for us amazing? He sends the rain, which waters the earth so plants can grow. Thank you, God, for rain!

name

Trace the words "Thank you, God, for rain!"

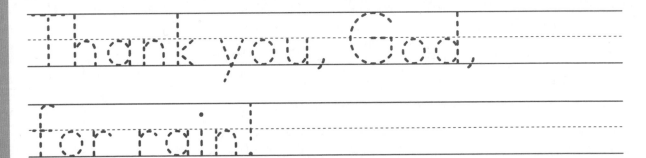

God brings rain! Let's color the picture .

Discussion Starters ▶

What is condensation, evaporation, and precipitation?

Rain is one way God cares for the earth. Can you think of any other ways He cares for us?

Let's memorize

Psalm 147:7–8 (NIrV)

"**Sing** to the Lord and give him grateful **praise**. Make **music to our God on the harp**. He **covers** the sky with clouds. He supplies the earth with **rain**. He makes grass grow on the **hills**."

	Actions
Sing	Place your hands around your mouth, as if you are going to call for someone loudly. You can also say this word in a sing-song voice.
praise	Put your hands together like you are praying or raise your hands in worship.
music to our God on the harp	Pretend to play the harp or another instrument.
covers	Lift your hands above your head with your palms facing the sky. Spread them apart as if they are moving across something that covers the sky.
rain	Wiggle your fingers and move your hands down, as if it is raining.
hills	Trace hills in the air with your pointer finger.

Experience

materials needed

- ☐ Mason jar or large glass cup
- ☐ Shaving cream
- ☐ Blue food coloring
- ☐ Water
- ☐ Small bowl
- ☐ Dropper or spoon
- ☐ Plastic bag or a flat plate (to protect surface)

Today, we are going to make rain in a jar. It will be so much fun! We learned about precipitation in our last lesson — that is what we call it when it rains. What are we waiting for? Let's get started!

Activity directions:

1. Fill a jar about halfway full of water.

2. Spray a layer of shaving cream above the water to look like a cloud. For less mess, do not spray shaving cream to the top of the jar. Leave a little gap between the top of the jar and the top of the shaving cream "cloud."

3. Add water to a small bowl and add a drop or two of blue food coloring.

4. Instruct student to use dropper or spoon to slowly drop water on top of the shaving cream cloud. When the cloud becomes too full of water, it will begin to rain out the bottom of the cloud!

5. Watch it rain in the jar.

Wow! You made rain in a jar. That was so cool to see! Water evaporates from the earth — from streams, ponds, lakes, and the ocean. The water vapor floats through the sky until it is up high where it is colder. It then condenses to form clouds. Then, the water droplets in the clouds stick to each other until they become too heavy, and the water drop falls back to the earth as rain, hail, sleet, or snow.

Some of the rainwater will sink deep into the ground, and some of the rainwater will go back to streams, ponds, lakes, or oceans where it will evaporate again. We call this the water cycle. Isn't it neat? God designed an amazing system to recycle water and care for the earth. Rain is a very special part of God's creation.

Discussion Starters

Can you tell me about the water cycle?

What happens when the water droplets become too big and heavy in the cloud?

Share

Tear out for Science Notebook

name

Whew — what a week it has been! We learned about precipitation. Do you remember what that is? Precipitation is rain! We were able to make rain in a jar, and then we learned about the water cycle. We've come to the end of our week, and now it's time to share what we have learned! Are you ready?

God made the water cycle! Let's color the picture of how it works.

Trace the words from Psalm 147:7-8 (NIrV) below.

Sing to the Lord and give him grateful praise. Make music to our God on the harp.

He covers the sky with clouds. He supplies the earth with rain. He makes grass grow on the hills.

Thunderstorms

2nd Day of Creation

Day

Learn

Drip, drop, drip, drop, drip, drop . . . can you hear it raining with your imagination? It's raining faster now! Drip, drop, drip, drop, drip, drop — crash! Ooh, listen — off in the distance, there is thunder! This week, we are learning about thunderstorms. Have you ever had a thunderstorm where you live?

What was it like?

Did you hear thunder and see the lightning?

How did you feel?

Thunderstorms can feel a bit scary, but they are also a neat part of God's creation. Thunderstorms clean the air for us and help to create soil that plants can grow well in. Are you ready to learn more about them? Let's get started!

Remember when we learned about clouds? There are three basic types of clouds: cumulus, stratus, and cirrus. Cumulus clouds are puffy and fluffy — like cotton candy in the sky. Sometimes, the air around us has lots of water vapor floating in it. We call this moist or humid air. When the air is warm and humid, a cumulus cloud can begin to grow very fast.

The warm, humid air rises fast, and the water droplets begin to cool — condense — in the

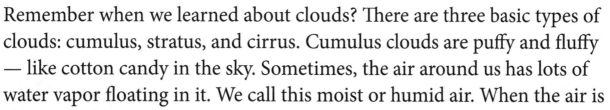

Balloon	✓
Fork	
Fleece (optional)	

Weekly materials list

colder air inside the cumulus cloud. As more and more water vapor condenses, the cloud begins to grow taller and taller. Soon, the cumulus cloud is very tall. It may even reach up to the stratosphere! When we see a cumulus cloud that looks like a head of cauliflower growing tall, or a cloud that reaches tall into the atmosphere and has a flat top, we call this a cumulonimbus cloud or a thunderhead.

Air passes through the cloud, carrying droplets of water that travel high up in the cloud. We call this the updraft. The updraft helps to keep the rain, and maybe even hail, floating inside the cloud. Remember, the warm air is becoming cooler inside the cloud as the water condenses, and eventually, the rain and hail will become too heavy for the updraft winds to hold up. When this happens, it will begin to rain or hail very hard.

The rain or hail will pull the cold air down out of the cloud very quickly. This is called the downdraft, and it can create very strong winds as the cold air falls out of the cloud rapidly and hits the ground. We may also see lightning and hear thunder. We'll talk more about those in our next lesson!

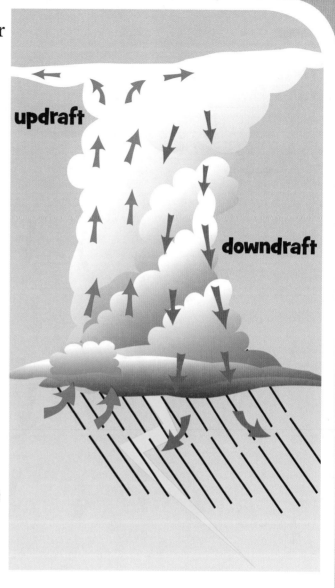

As it rains very hard, the updraft is still trying to pull warm air into the cloud to help it grow, while the downdraft is pushing everything back down and out of the cloud. The downdraft will eventually be stronger than the updraft, and warm air will stop flowing into the cloud to create more rain. Then, the cloud will begin to become smaller, and the rain will fall more slowly until the thunderstorm is all over.

Sometimes, the cloud is tipped a little bit on its side. This makes it harder for the downdraft to be stronger than the updraft, so the cloud can continue to make rain for more time. These types of thunderstorms can last for a longer time, but most storms last for about 30 to 60 minutes.

Thunderstorms release a lot of water very quickly. They help to provide water to plants, animals, and people. The raindrops help clean the air, and lightning also helps the plants. We'll learn more about that in our next lesson!

name

Trace the words.

updraft

downdraft

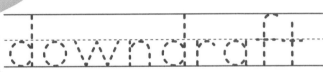

Discussion Starters

Can you tell me how a thunderstorm forms?

What is the updraft?

What is the downdraft?

Experience

materials needed

- ☐ Balloon
- ☐ Fork
- ☐ Fleece (optional)

Have you ever seen lightning in the sky? It's pretty amazing, isn't it? Lightning is made of static electricity. Today, we are going to make some mini-lightning of our own. What do you think, are you ready to try it? Let's get started!

Have you ever rubbed a balloon across your hair? The balloon rubbing across your hair creates static electricity, and this is like how lightning is formed. The water droplets, hail, and ice inside a cloud bounce around and rub against each other. This creates static electricity, which fills up the cloud. Static electricity is made of positive charges and negative charges. The positive charges stay at the top of the cloud while the negative charges settle at the bottom.

When there is enough electrical charge in the cloud, all the energy needs to go somewhere — so lightning flashes through the sky! The electrical energy will travel to a place that has the opposite electrical charge, so usually the lightning will hit another cloud or something like a tree on the ground.

Remember when we studied light and learned about light waves? The sounds we hear also travel through the air in a wave pattern. Lightning rips apart the air around it, and then the air comes back together. Thunder is the sound wave that is created when the air splits apart and comes back together. Isn't that neat?

Lightning also has a special purpose. It changes nitrogen (which is a gas in the atmosphere) to nitrous oxide. The nitrous oxide the lightning created will then fall to the dirt where plants can use it.

Have you ever touched something and felt a little spark on your fingers? That is static electricity, just like lightning! Do you want to try to make some of our own lightning? I do! Let's give it a try!

Activity directions:

1. Blow up the balloon and then go into a dark room.

2. Place the fork on a flat surface.

3. Rub the balloon quickly over your hair or a piece of fleece to create static electricity. Once the balloon is statically charged, move it slowly toward the fork until they touch.

4. You should see a small spark of light between the two. If you don't, rotate the balloon slightly and touch it again a couple of times. Repeat as many times as you'd like!

That was so cool! Did you see the spark between the fork and the balloon? That spark was made of static electricity, just like lightning in the sky. Of course, lightning in the sky is much, much bigger than the spark we created with our balloon. Lightning and thunder can feel a bit scary because there is so much light and noise!

The Bible has a lot of verses that talk about fear and feeling afraid. Let's read one of those special verses!

So do not fear, for I am with you; do not be dismayed, for I am your God. I will strengthen you and help you; I will uphold you with my righteous right hand (Isaiah 41:10).

That is a good verse to remember when you feel afraid. God made lightning, and He is much more powerful than it. We can trust Him when we are afraid — even when it is stormy outside.

Discussion Starters

What are some times when you are afraid?

What can you remember when you are afraid?

Discuss storm safety with your student:

- If you are outside and hear thunder or see lightning, come inside right away.

- Stay back from windows and doors during the storm.

- Don't take a shower or bath until the storm has passed.

Let your student guide a friend or family member through this activity and make lightning.

Let's memorize

Isaiah 41:10

"So do not **fear**, for I am with you; do not be **dismayed**, for I am your God. I will **strengthen** you and help you; I will uphold you with my righteous **right hand**."

	Actions
fear	Place your hands over your face, as if you are afraid.
dismayed	Drop your arms to your sides and shrug your shoulders.
strengthen	Put your arms up and show your muscles!
right hand	Raise your right hand up.

Day

Share

name

Today is the day we get to share what we've learned about thunderstorms and add a page to our Science Notebook! This is a picture of a thunderstorm. Can you draw your own picture of a thunderstorm with lightning? Then, we'll trace our verse to remind us that God is with us, and we don't have to be afraid — even in the storms.

Tear out for Science Notebook

name

Color the thunderstorm.

Draw your own thunderstorm!

Do you remember Isaiah 41:10? Trace it and then let's say it together!

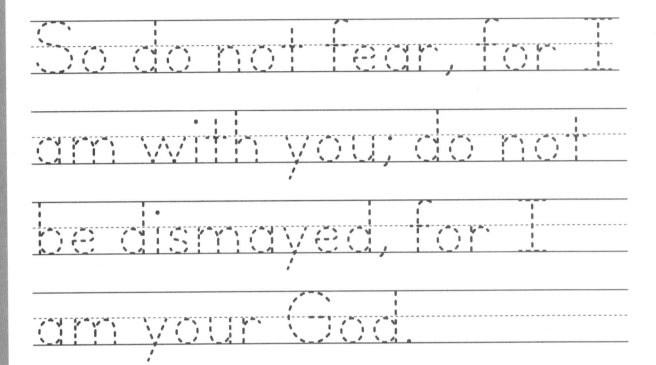

So do not fear, for I
am with you; do not
be dismayed, for I
am your God.

The Third Day of Creation

3rd Day of Creation

Day

Learn

I'm so excited to start a new week of science with you! Can you remember what we learned in our last few lessons? Hmm, what did God make on the first day of creation? God made the heavens, earth, and light on the first day of creation! We've learned that light travels fast, that it is made of colors, and that it travels in waves. We even learned about the rainbow!

Do you remember what God made on the second day of creation? God made the sky — the atmosphere — on day two! We learned about the layers of the atmosphere, about condensation and evaporation, clouds, the water cycle, and thunderstorms. We've had quite an adventure through creation so far.

I wonder what God made on the third day of creation? Do you wonder, too? Where do you think we should take our questions? [Allow student to answer.]

That's right, to the Bible! Let's read about the third day of creation in Genesis 1:9–13 (NIrV):

God said, "Let the water under the sky be gathered into one place. Let dry ground appear." And that's exactly what happened. God called the dry ground "land." He called all the water that was gathered together "seas." And God saw that it was good.

Then God said, "Let the land produce plants. Let them produce their own seeds. And let there be trees on the land that grow fruit with seeds in it. Let each kind of plant or tree have its own kind of seeds." And that's exactly what happened. So the land produced plants. Each kind of plant had its own kind of seeds. And the land produced trees that grew fruit with seeds in it. Each kind of tree had its own kind of seeds. God saw that it was good. There was evening, and there was morning. It was day three.

I think we heard our answer in those verses. Did you hear it, too? What did God make on the third day of creation? [Dry ground and plants.]

We learned that God created the earth on the first day of creation and that the earth was covered in water. The earth wasn't ready yet because God was going to continue creating. Then, on the third day of creation, God created dry ground on the earth and plants. How amazing!

We're going to explore the land and plants together in our next few lessons. Let's start with land. On the third day, God separated the water on the earth, and He created dry ground. We live on the earth, on dry ground. The earth is very big, and it has large areas of dry ground, or land, that we call "continents," and large areas of water that we call "seas" or "oceans."

The Bible says that when God created land, all of the water was gathered into one place and dry ground appeared. During creation, God may have created one really big ocean and one really big area of land. We call this a continent. The earth looks a bit different today, though. Now, we see seven large areas of land — or continents — on the earth.

Do you remember when we learned about the rainbow and the Flood that happened when Noah was alive? The Flood changed the earth in many ways, and it may have broken apart the really big area of land God created and formed the many smaller areas of land we see today.

I wonder if Adam and Eve ever asked God about the third day of creation. Let's imagine they did. In our last story, Cain, Abel, and Adam had learned about rain. Let's imagine what happened next.

Imagine That!
Bible-inspired stories

Later that day, the rain had stopped, and Adam, Eve, Cain, and Abel sat inside their tent eating a yummy dinner. "Mom?" Abel asked. "We've learned what God created on the first and second days of creation. What did God make on the third day?"

"Ah, yes," Eve answered. "Well, you remember that on the first day of creation, God made the earth, and it was covered in water. On the third day of creation, God gathered the water together in one place, and He made dry land. Then God made plants to grow on the dry land."

"We live on the dry land, right Mom?" Cain asked.

"Yes, we do — along with the animals, but God made the animals, and your dad and me, later on," answered Eve.

"Can you teach us about land and plants, Mom and Dad?" asked Cain.

"Yes, we would love to!" both Adam and Eve answered.

"Plants are also a really neat part of God's creation. We'll talk more about them soon. Let's clean up after dinner first," Eve said, and they all worked together to tidy things up.

I'm so excited to explore land and plants with you! The earth today has seven continents — or large areas of land. We're going to learn more about that in our next lesson.

name

Trace the words. Color the picture.

God made land and
plants.

Discussion Starters ►

What did God make on the third day of creation?

What do we call a large area of land?

Is this how God originally created things?

Sin and the Flood changed God's original creation. Think of some things that are different and discuss them with your child. For instance, because of sin, we see disease and sad things happen.

Day ••

Experience

materials needed

☐ Crayons, colored pencils, or markers

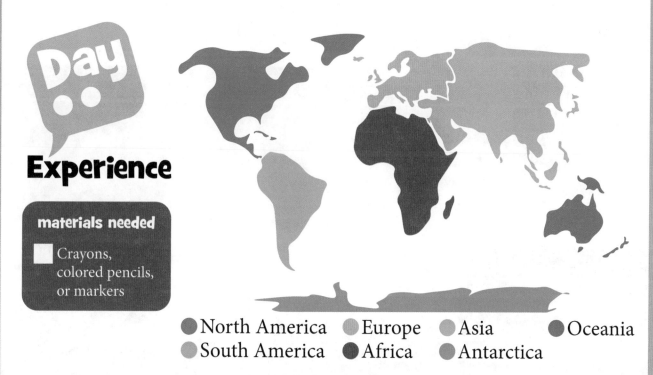

● North America ● Europe ● Asia ● Oceania
● South America ● Africa ● Antarctica

Which continent do you live on? Can you point to it on the map above?

There are different types of land on each continent. Some places have mountains, others are very flat. Some places have very good soil, some have sand, and others have very hard soil or rocks. Other places are covered in ice and snow! Some continents have a little bit of everything.

Teacher Tip: Sometimes when discussing the continents, instead of mentioning just Australia, books will refer to the area of Oceania. It consists of the number of islands in addition to Australia.

Depending on the weather, you may also go outside with your student and explore the terrain and dirt around your house or community.

Discussion Starters

What does the land look like in your area?

Have you traveled to another area that is different?

What was the land like there?

Do you have family members that live on a different continent?

How is it different where they live?

Would you like to live in an area with mountains or flat land?

Would you like to live next to the ocean or far away from it?

Do you like dry weather or lots of rainy weather?

name

What kind of land do you live on? Are there mountains, is it flat, or somewhere in between? What kind of dirt do you have? Is it dry and rocky, sandy, or good for growing a garden in?

Let's draw a picture of what the land looks like around your house and thank God for the land He gave us to live on.

Where do you live and what is it like?
Your teacher can help you fill in the blanks.

I live in ——————————————————— [your continent]

My address is ——————————————— [your address]

I live in ————————————————[country or city]

The weather is ——————————— [describe weather]

My favorite thing to do is ———————————————

Day

Share

We've covered a lot of ground this week! This week, we learned about what God created on the third day of creation. Do you remember what it was? He made land and plants on the third day! We've also learned a little bit about continents — the large areas of land on the earth — and we observed the land around us.

name

Today, we want to share what we've learned with someone! Let's color a map of the seven continents — the land God created — and circle the continent you live on. In our next lesson, we'll get to learn about what the earth looks like on the inside, and I can hardly wait! Don't forget to share with someone what you've learned this week — that God created dry ground.

Color the continents the correct color.

● North America   ● South America   ● Oceania/Australia   ● Antarctica

● Asia   ● Africa   ● Europe

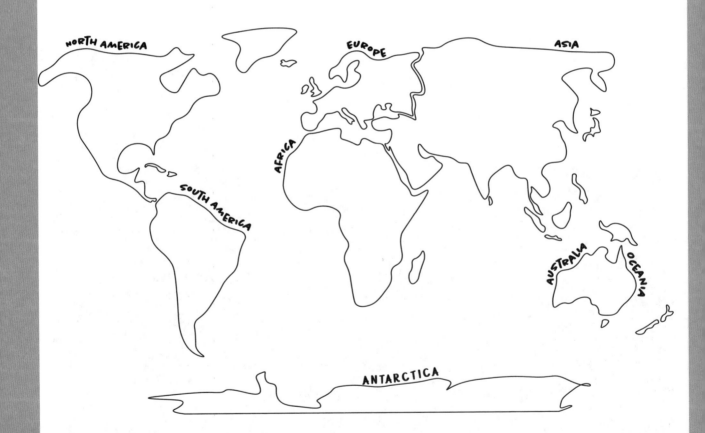

Earth Layers

3rd Day of Creation

Day Learn

Are you ready for another science adventure? Last week, we looked at the dry land — the continents — under our feet, but I wonder what is under the dry ground we see. Do you wonder, too? Today, we'll explore what is inside the earth. Let's get started!

The earth is made of layers deep inside that we can't see. Sometimes, the continents move around a little bit and it causes the land to rumble and shake. We call this an earthquake. Scientists study the vibrations from earthquakes to learn what the earth may be made of under the surface we can see. From those studies, scientists believe the earth has four layers: the crust, mantle, outer core, and inner core.

The crust is the layer we live on. It has the oceans and continents. This is the layer that we can study, experience, and see for ourselves. However, even this layer is too thick to drill a hole all the way through! The crust is thicker in some places and thinner in others. It depends on whether there is land or ocean covering that spot. The crust can be just under 4 miles thick under the deepest parts of the ocean — or 56 miles thick under the highest mountains on land!

Playdough in 4 colors	✓
Butter knife	☐
Glue stick	☐
Scissors	☐

Weekly materials list

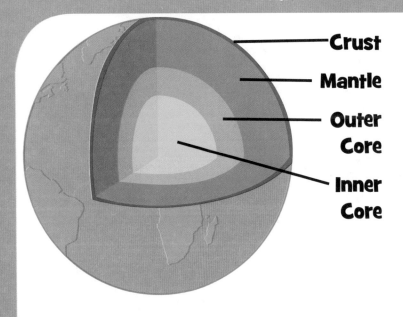

Crust
Mantle
Outer Core
Inner Core

The next layer inside the earth is called the mantle. This layer is made of rock that is being pressed very hard by the weight of the earth, so nothing can live deep inside the earth in this layer. The mantle is about 1,802 miles thick, and it is very, very hot.

Below the mantle is the core deep within the center of the earth. Scientists believe there is an outer core and an inner core hidden inside the outer core. We believe the outer core is made of liquid sulfur and iron. This layer is extremely hot! Inside the outer core, there is an inner core that is made of solid iron. The inner core is the hottest layer.

God's creation is so amazing! We may not know for sure exactly what the inside of the earth is made of or what it looks like since it is so deep within the earth, but God created it, so we know that He does! In Psalm 95:1–5, we read:

Come, let us sing for joy to the LORD; let us shout aloud to the Rock of our salvation. Let us come before him with thanksgiving and extol him with music and song. For the LORD is the great God, the great King above all gods. In his hand are the depths of the earth and the mountain peaks belong to him. The sea is his, for he made it, and his hands formed the dry land.

God gave us the ability to learn, study, and explore His world. One way we study His world is through science. As we study and learn more about His creation, it reminds us that God is amazing — that He is our Creator. Science reminds us that we don't know everything, but we know God does because He is the one who made it. Science reminds us to praise and thank God for His care of us.

name

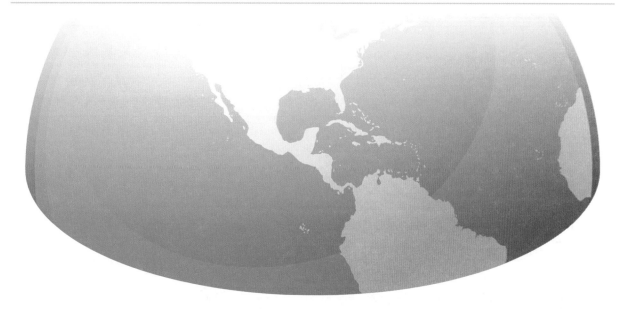

Let's color the layers of the earth!

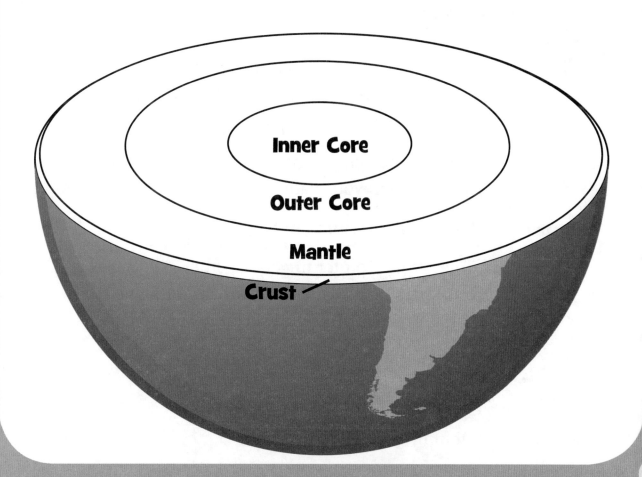

Inner Core

Outer Core

Mantle

Crust

Trace Psalm 95:4.

In his hand are the
depths of the earth,
and the mountain
peaks belong to him.

Let's memorize
Psalm 95:4–5

"In his **hand** are the depths of the **earth**, and the **mountain** peaks belong to him. The **sea** is his, for he made it, and his **hands** formed the dry **land**."

	Actions
hand	Hold up one cupped hand, as if you are holding something in your palm.
earth	Form a circle with both hands.
mountain	Touch your pointer fingers together at eye level and trace a triangle shape in the air as you move your hands down at an angle and then back together.
sea	Use your hands to make waves in the air.
hands	Cup both hands together.
land	Stomp your feet on the floor.

Day

Experience

materials needed

☐ Playdough in 4 colors

☐ Butter knife

We've been learning about the layers of the earth. Would you like to make a model of the layers? Let's get started! First, we'll need to make the inner core. Pick out one color of playdough and form it into a small ball. This is our inner core.

Next, pick out another color of playdough and form a ball just a bit bigger than the first ball — then, smoosh it flat! Once it is flat, wrap the first small ball in this layer. This is our outer core, which covers the inner core.

Pick a third color and follow that same process. Form a slightly bigger ball, squish it flat, and wrap it around the inner and outer core. Now we've made the mantle.

Finally, grab the last color and squish it flat. This will be our crust. Wrap the ball up in this color. We've made our model of the earth! But now we want to see those layers on the inside. Ask your teacher to cut the ball in half. Now you can see the crust, the mantle, the inner core, and the outer core that you made!

God created the earth and the layers inside. We may not know exactly what those layers are made of or what they look like, but God does. In the Bible, there is the story of a man named Job. Job loved God with all his heart, but then very, very sad things happened to Job. Job was really sad and wondered why those bad things happened. Then, God spoke to Job. God didn't tell Job why those bad things happened, though. Instead, God asked Job many questions, and Job learned that God is wise and powerful. Let's read one of the questions God asked Job!

"Where were you when I laid the earth's foundation? Tell me, if you know. Who measured it? I am sure you know! Who stretched a measuring line across it? What was it built on? Who laid its most important stone? When it happened, the morning stars sang together. All the angels shouted with joy" (Job 38:4–7; NIrV).

The layers of the earth remind us that God is wise and powerful — that He was there at the very beginning, and He knows how things work together. God cares for us, and we can trust Him even when we don't completely understand.

Discussion Starters

Can you think of a way you can trust God?

It's good to study creation because it teaches us and reminds us about God. What is something you'd like to study in creation?

Who made the earth and the layers deep inside it?

Day **Share**

What an adventure we've had this week through the layers of the earth! Today, it's time to add another page to our Science Notebook and share what we've learned with someone else. Let's put together the layers of the earth!

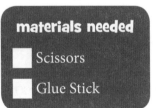

materials needed
- Scissors
- Glue Stick

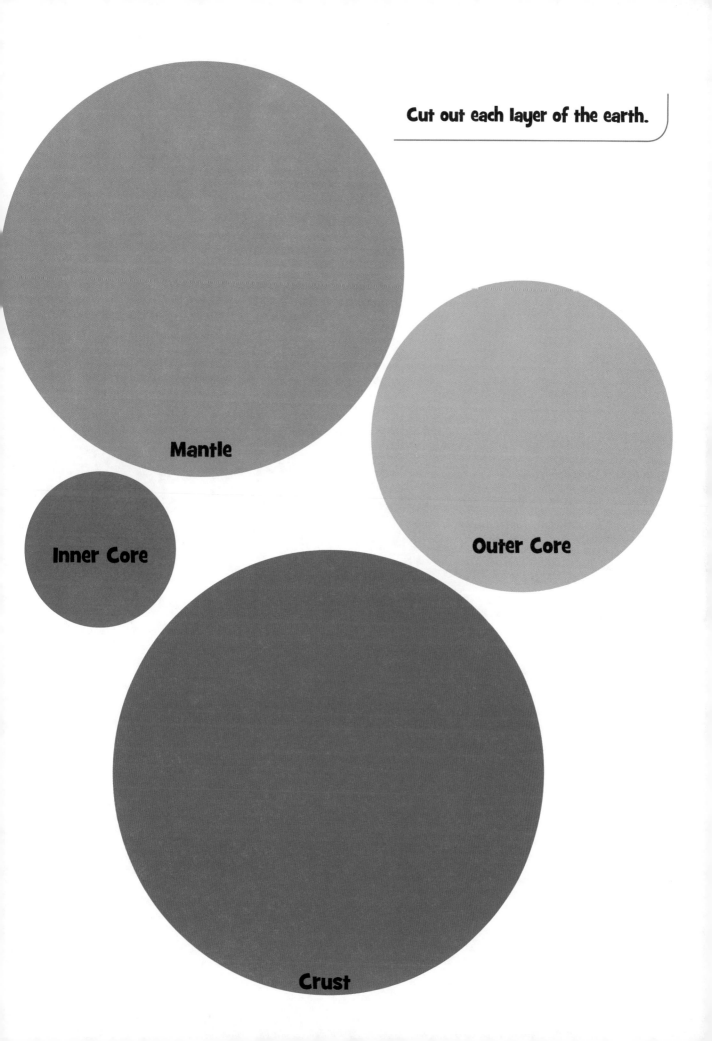

Cut out each layer of the earth.

Mantle

Outer Core

Inner Core

Crust

Blank for cutting circles.

name

Glue the crust below. On top of the crust, glue the mantle. Glue the outer core on top of the mantle, and then the inner core on top of the outer core.

Blank for gluing.

Plants

3rd Day of Creation

Learn

Do you remember what God made on the third day of creation? [Allow student to answer. Answer should be dry land and plants.] God made dry land and plants on the third day of creation! We've explored dry land and what is underneath the land under our feet. Now it's time to talk about what grows in and on the land God made.

On the third day of creation, God made plants. Can you think of some plants? [Allow student to answer.] There are flowers, grasses, shrubs, bushes, trees, and so many more kinds of plants! Some plants produce food for us to eat, others do not. What is your favorite kind of plant? [Allow student to answer.]

Hmm, I have a question. What keeps plants in the dirt? How do the tall trees stay standing, and the grass not blow away in the wind? Do you wonder, too?

Let's talk about plants today and the special ways God created them. In our last story, Cain and Abel learned about the third day of creation, and they were helping to clean up after dinner. Let's imagine what happened next as they learned about plants!

Stalks of celery, with leaves	✓
Glass jar	
Food coloring	
Scissors	

Weekly materials list

Bible-inspired stories

Adam, Eve, Cain, and Abel cleaned up after dinner and got ready for bed that night. The air got a little colder, and the wind began to blow strongly. Abel heard the rustle of the leaves blowing in the strong wind. He was a little scared.

"Dad, what is that sound?" Abel asked as he climbed into Adam's lap.

"That is the wind, buddy. It is blowing strongly tonight."

"I'm a little scared, Dad."

Adam hugged Abel tight as he thought back to the Garden of Eden. He had never been afraid there, until he sinned. Sin had broken the world, and now Adam knew what it was like to feel afraid.

But, he also remembered what it was like to walk and talk with God and how much God cared for him and Eve, even after they sinned. Adam hugged Abel tight. "I feel afraid sometimes too, Abel, but it helps to remember how much God loves us and that He cares for us. Even when we can't see Him or understand what is happening," Adam said softly.

Abel prayed and thanked God for watching over them. Then, they all went to bed, and the wind blew all that night.

Soon it was morning, and after breakfast, Adam and Abel walked to the fields to check on their flocks. Abel saw a small, young tree lying on the ground. The wind had been too strong for the young tree, and it had blown over. "Dad, what are those funny looking things at the end of the tree, all covered in dirt?" Abel giggled.

"Those are the roots of the tree. The roots are like fingers that dig into the ground and hold on tight. The tree's roots help it stay standing tall. It doesn't look like this tree had strong roots yet, so it blew over in the wind," Adam replied as Abel touched the roots.

"The roots help the plant or tree stay standing. Plants and trees also use their roots to absorb water and nutrients — which is like food for the plant — from the dirt. The plant uses its roots to draw in the water and nutrients it needs and pull them into the stem — this part right here," Adam said as he pointed out the trunk of the tree. "Then the stem sends the water and nutrients to the rest of the plant."

"Wow! I didn't know that!" said Abel.

Adam laughed. "There is a lot we can learn about God's creation, son, and there are many lessons creation can teach us. God takes care of the plants, and He takes care of us, too." Then, Adam and Abel continued walking to the field, looking at different plants and talking about how God cares for them.

Have you ever picked a plant or a flower from outside and seen the roots at the end of the plant? What did they look like?

133

Roots can look different, depending on what kind of plant it is. Some plants, like many flowers and grass, have many tiny roots growing in every direction. These are called fibrous roots.

Other plants grow one large root, and smaller roots grow out from the large root. This is called a taproot. A carrot is a type of taproot.

People can eat fruits from some plants, sometimes the plant itself, and even some types of roots — like carrots.

Tree roots are thick. You may even be able to see some of the roots above the ground. Tree roots may grow down very deep or spread very wide. The tree's roots help it stand tall and strong. I'm excited to learn more about roots this week with you!

name

God designed plants with a root system to help anchor the plant in the dirt, and also to help them receive water and nutrients from the soil. Look at the example for each plant, then finish drawing the roots for each picture.

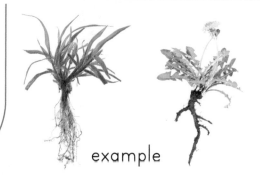

example

example

Discussion Starters

Have you ever seen a fallen tree?

What did the roots look like?

What type of root system do you see?

Can you think of any other root vegetables you eat?

If the weather allows, go outside and pull some plants out of the dirt.

Experience

materials needed

- ☐ Stalks of celery, with leaves
- ☐ Glass jar
- ☐ Food coloring
- ☐ Water

Teacher Tip:
Observations for the following experiment will take place over two days. After the initial set-up, proceed with the rest of the lesson, coming back later for your student to note changes as indicated in the activity directions.

We're learning about plants and how their roots and stems draw in water and nutrients to feed the plant or tree. We're going to start an experiment today to watch how the stem of a plant works. The roots of a plant act a bit like a straw. They help the plant draw in water and nutrients. Roots draw in water, but so can the stem if there are no roots. That's how flowers can stay alive for a little while in a glass of water when we pick them.

Celery has a stem, and it can draw in water even without roots. We're going to put some celery into a glass with colored water. What do you think will happen? [Allow student time to answer.]

You think _____ .
[fill in with student's answer]

Do you remember what this is called? What you think will happen is your hypothesis! Let's get started.

Activity directions:

1. Take a few stalks of celery and cut off the bottom wide part of the stalk.

2. Fill a glass with water and add several drops of food coloring. Blue or red is a great color to use.

3. Place the stalks of celery in the glass.
   Optional: You can fill several glasses of water and color them differently. Then, add stalks of celery to each glass to observe the different colors.

Our celery experiment is all set up! Now, we'll keep an eye on our celery stalks over the next two days and watch what happens.

Day 1:

Observe the celery 4–6 hours later in the day. Have you noticed any changes?

Day 2:

Finally, observe the celery the following morning. Carefully remove the celery from the glass and cut off about a half-inch from the bottom.

> **What do you see?**

> **Can you see the color traveling through the veins of the celery?**

Did you know the Bible also talks about roots? It does! Colossians 2:6–7 (NIrV) tells us, *"You received Christ Jesus as Lord. So keep on living your lives in him. Have your roots in him. Build yourselves up in him. Grow strong in what you believe, just as you were taught. Be more thankful than ever before."*

The Bible reminds us to have our roots in God. What do you think that means? This is a way of saying that we need to keep learning and growing in our relationship with God. As we do, it is like building strong roots in our heart that keep us strong in Jesus. Then, just like the roots of a plant help it stand strong, the roots in your heart will help you stand strong with Jesus, too. When you think of roots, or when you see a root on a plant, remember that you can keep growing in your faith and grow strong roots in Jesus, too.

Discussion Starters

Go on a nature walk.

Can you find any tree roots above the ground?

Can you think of a way you can keep growing in Jesus?

Let's memorize

Colossians 2:6–7 (NIrV)

"You **received** Christ Jesus as Lord. So keep on **living** your lives in him. Have your **roots** in him. **Build** yourselves up in him. Grow **strong** in what you believe, just as you were taught. Be more **thankful** than ever before."

	Actions
received	Reach up with open hands, close your hands, and pull them toward you.
living	Walk in place.
roots	Stomp your feet.
Build	Make two fists and stack them, one on top of the other as if building a tower.
strong	Show your muscles!
thankful	Place your hands together to pray.

Share

Today's the day! It's time to add a new page to our Science Notebook! Hey, how does your celery look from our experiment? What happened? [Allow student to answer.]

Is that what you thought would happen? [Allow student to answer.]

We were able to see the plant draw in water and move it through the stem to the leaves. That's why the plant changed color a little. It was moving our colored water through itself. That's how God designed it.

Are you ready to share what we've learned about plant roots? Let's draw roots on the tree on the next page and trace Colossians 2:6–7 to remind us to grow strong roots in God. Be sure to tell someone how God made plants with roots to hold them secure and draw food and water from the soil!

name

Draw roots on this tree.

Trace Colossians 2:6-7 (NIrV)

You received Christ
Jesus as Lord. So
keep on living your
lives in him. Have
your roots in him.

Trace and color.

Leaves and Photosynthesis

3rd Day of Creation

Day

Learn

Hello friend, are you ready for another science adventure? We're learning about the third day of creation when God made land and plants. We've already learned about land, and last week we learned about plant roots and the stem. Now, what about the leaves of a plant? I'd like to learn a little more about leaves. How about you? Put on your scientist goggles, and let's explore them!

The roots of a plant draw in water and nutrients for the plant, then the stem moves the water and nutrients up through the plant to the leaves. Leaves have a special job. What do you think it is? [Allow student to answer.]

Let's talk about the special job God gave to leaves! Leaves have something called chlorophyll inside them. Can you say that word with me? Chlorophyll. Chlorophyll is what causes leaves to be green, and it has a very important job. Leaves have water from the ground inside them. Remember the stem brought them water? Leaves also absorb a gas called carbon dioxide from the air around them. Take a deep breath in, and now breathe it out. When you breathe out, you exhale. Exhale is a fancy word that means breathe out. When you exhale, you breathe out carbon dioxide — the same gas the plant absorbs!

Magnifying glass	✓
Various leaves from outside. May also use spinach or leaves from grocery store flowers.	☐
Paper	☐
Crayons	☐

Weekly materials list

143

When the sun shines on the leaf, something amazing happens. Chlorophyll uses the sunlight to create sugar and oxygen from the water and carbon dioxide inside the leaf. The plant releases the oxygen into the air so that people and animals can breathe it in. Chlorophyll in leaves helps to produce clean air for us to breathe. Then, the plant uses the sugar that was also created and holds it inside the fruit and the rest of the plant.

We call this photosynthesis! What a big word, but it's fun to say! Can you say it with me? Photosynthesis. Photosynthesis is what happens when chlorophyll uses the sunlight to create sugar and oxygen from the water and carbon dioxide inside a leaf.

Isn't God's creation amazing? God made a special relationship between plants and animals and people. Animals and people exhale — breathe out — carbon dioxide. The plant needs carbon dioxide to make food for itself. The plant absorbs the carbon dioxide and makes oxygen that people and animals need to inhale — breathe in.

Have you ever looked closely at a leaf? There are many shapes and sizes, and there are tiny lines we can see. These are called veins. The leaf uses the veins to move water and sugar around. We'll look a little closer at veins in our next lesson!

name

Photosynthesis is a special job God gave the leaves on plants. Trace the words (ask your teacher to read them to you).

carbon
dioxide

oxygen

light

water

145

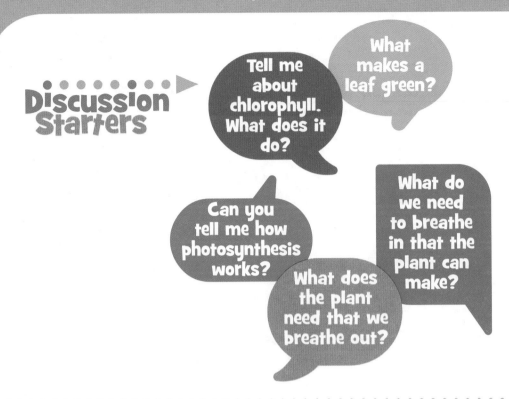

Discussion Starters

Tell me about chlorophyll. What does it do?

What makes a leaf green?

Can you tell me how photosynthesis works?

What do we need to breathe in that the plant can make?

What does the plant need that we breathe out?

Day ..

Experience

materials needed

☐ Magnifying glass

☐ Various leaves from outside. May also use spinach or leaves from grocery store flowers.

☐ Paper

☐ Crayons

Are you ready to look a little more closely at leaves? In our last lesson, we learned that leaves use a process called photosynthesis to create sugar and oxygen. If we look closely at leaves, we can also see a pattern of lines. These are called veins. The leaf uses the veins to transport sugar and water through the plant.

Look at the leaf very closely. Do you see the pattern of lines? Use the magnifying glass to make them a little bigger. Tell me about the veins you see. What do they look like?

Now let's look at another leaf. First, look with just your eyes. What do you see? Do the veins look the same as the first leaf or is the pattern a little different? Then, look at the leaf under the magnifying glass and tell me about what you see.

Let's put one of the leaves under a piece of paper and use a crayon to gently color over the top of it. Do you see any of the leaf veins in the leaf drawing? Trace over the veins in the drawing to make them a little darker. You can try to color another leaf on the same sheet of paper or a different one if you'd like!

The veins in a leaf help the water and sugar get to where it needs to go in a plant. God designed plants with an amazing system of veins that help the plant take care of itself. So far, we've learned about roots, stems, and the leaves on a plant, but we have more things to learn about plants in our next few lessons. I can hardly wait!

Discussion Starters

Go on a nature walk.

How many different shapes and sizes of leaves can you find?

What do the veins look like on different leaves?

Do you see different patterns?

Can you draw the stem of the plant to connect all the leaves?

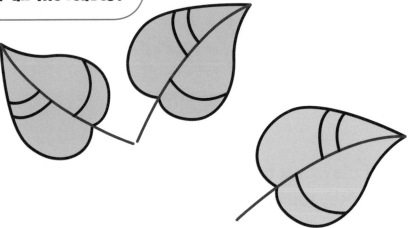

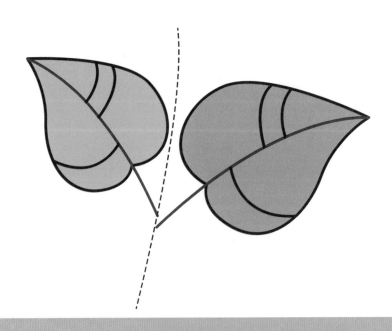

Share

name

We got to study leaves and photosynthesis this week. What was your favorite part? Today, it's time to add a new page to your Science Notebook! Through photosynthesis, leaves make sugar and oxygen. The veins in a leaf help the plant move water and sugar to where it needs to go.

Don't forget to tell someone all about the amazing way God designed leaves as you add this page to your Science Notebook.

Let's complete the maze! Help the caterpillar eat its way through the leaf.

Draw a picture of plants and the sun — don't forget to add leaves to the plants!

Flowers and Pollination

3rd Day of Creation

Day

Learn

We're learning about the third day of creation, do you remember what God made on day three? [Allow student to answer.] God made dry land and plants!

We've learned about the continents and the layers inside the earth. Next we learned about roots, leaves, and photosynthesis. Can you tell me about leaves and photosynthesis? [Allow student to answer.]

God made the parts of a plant to work together to keep the plant strong and healthy. Can you think of something else some plants have? They are colorful and come in many shapes, sizes, and colors. Can you think of what it is? Flowers!

Some plants and trees have flowers. Flowers are colorful and very pretty, but they also have a very important job. Flowers help the plant create seeds that will later grow into new plants. Without flowers, we wouldn't have any new plants. God sure is an amazing designer!

I'm sure Cain and Abel saw many beautiful flowers. Do you think they ever talked to Adam about how flowers work? Let's imagine they did!"

Flour	✓
Cheetos®	☐
Cocoa powder	☐
Light, fuzzy winter gloves	☐
3 pieces of construction paper	☐
Crayons or markers	☐
Pom-poms	☐
Elmer's glue®	☐

Weekly materials list

Bible-inspired stories

It was a nice day. The sun was bright and warm. Adam, Eve, Cain, and Abel decided to go for a walk to explore creation. As they walked, Cain noticed many flowers along the path. Some flowers were big, some flowers were small. Some had bright colors, others were not so bright. There were flowers in all shapes, sizes, and colors!

"Dad, can you tell me about flowers? There are so many, and they are pretty. I'd like to learn about them," said Cain.

"Yes, let's talk about flowers!" Adam replied. "God made plants on the third day of creation. Flowers have a special job. They help the plant make seeds. Flowers have four things that work together. First, there are petals. These are often brightly colored and can feel soft," Adam explained.

Cain and Abel softly brushed their hand over a petal. "It feels so smooth!" they said together.

"Yes, it does. Here, look underneath the petals. Do you see those tiny leaves underneath? They help to protect the flower before it opens up. We call this part sepals."

Adam picked a brightly colored flower. There were long stems coming out of the middle of the flower, and the ends were covered in something that looked powdery. "Here, touch the end," Adam directed Cain and Abel. "These are called stamens, and they make pollen. Do you see the pollen on your fingers now?" Cain and Abel giggled as they looked at their fingers. They had pollen on them!

Adam pointed to the next part of the flower. "This part is called the pistil. It receives pollen from other plants, and then it makes seeds."

"Wow. There are many parts all working together in the flower," Abel said. He picked another flower and studied it closely.

"Boys, God takes care of the flowers in this field. They remind us that He is taking care of us, too," Adam said as they continued walking, looking at the beautiful flowers as they went.

Flowers are a beautiful part of God's creation, and they help the plant create new seeds that will grow into new plants. We'll learn about that a little more in our next lesson. Did you know there is a special place in the Bible that talks about flowers and reminds us not to worry? Let's read Matthew 6:25–34 (NIrV) where Jesus says,

I tell you, do not worry. Don't worry about your life and what you will eat or drink. And don't worry about your body and what you will wear. Isn't there more to life than eating? Aren't there more important things for the body than clothes? Look at the birds of the air. They don't plant or gather crops. They don't put away crops in storerooms. But your Father who is in heaven feeds them. Aren't you worth much more than they are? Can you add even one hour to your life by worrying?

And why do you worry about clothes? See how the wild flowers grow. They don't work or make clothing. But here is what I tell you. Not even Solomon in all his royal robes was dressed like one of these flowers. If that is how God dresses the wild grass, won't he dress you even better? Your faith is so small! After all, the grass is here only today. Tomorrow it is thrown into the fire. So don't worry. Don't say, "What will we eat?" Or, "What will we drink?" Or, "What will we wear?" People who are ungodly run after all those things. Your Father who is in heaven knows that you need them. But put God's kingdom first. Do what he wants you to do. Then all those things will also be given to you. So don't worry about tomorrow. Tomorrow will worry about itself. Each day has enough trouble of its own.

That was a lot to read, but it teaches us a very important lesson. God takes care of the birds and the wild flowers, and He knows what we need when we are following Him. When you see a flower, let it remind you that God takes care of the flowers in the field and that He takes care of you, too.

Discussion Starters

Purchase a bouquet of flowers from the grocery store and see if you can identify the petals, sepals, stamens, and pistil. Observe the leaves.

Can you also see the veins in the flower's leaf?

What is something you worry about or are scared of?

How do you think you can learn to trust God?

name

Trace the name for each part of the flower (ask your teacher to read them to you). Then, color the flower with your favorite color.

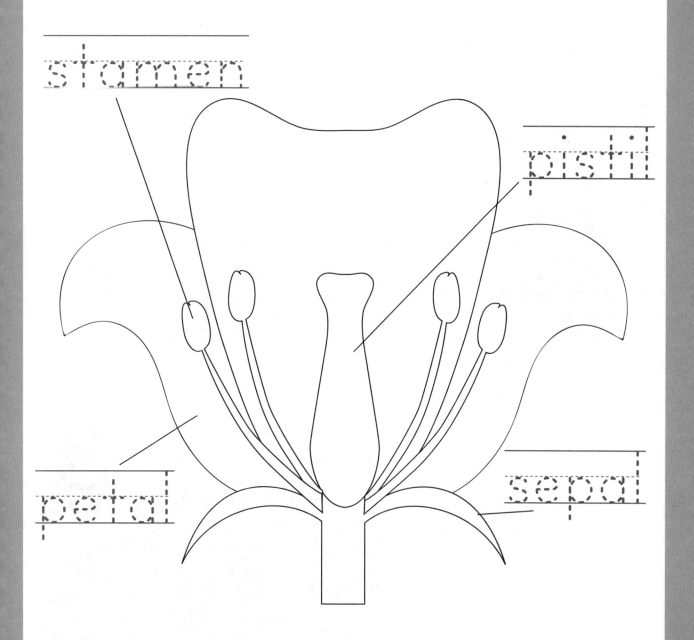

stamen

pistil

petal

sepal

Experience

materials needed

- ☐ Flour
- ☐ Cheetos®
- ☐ Cocoa powder
- ☐ Light, fuzzy winter gloves
- ☐ 3 pieces of construction paper
- ☐ Crayons or markers

In our last lesson, we got to learn about flowers. Do you remember any of the parts of a flower? [Allow student time to answer.] There are the petals in beautiful colors, the sepals that protect the flower, the stamen that makes pollen, and the pistil that takes pollen to make seeds. The pistil needs to receive pollen from another flower in order to make seeds. I wonder how the pistil gets pollen from a different flower? Do you wonder, too?

God made very special helpers for the pistil. Can you guess what they are? Bzzz, bzzz, bzzz, do you hear that noise? It sounds like a bee buzzing around us. Bees are one of the special helpers flowers have.

Bees are busy little insects. They fly around from flower to flower to flower. The flower creates nectar for the bee to drink. Nectar is sweet, and the brightly colored flower petals attract the bee to land on them to drink their yummy nectar. When the bee lands on the flower, it brushes up against the pollen on the stamen. The pollen sticks to the bee, then the bee flies off to another flower.

As the bee drinks from the new flower, some of the pollen from the first flower brushes off on the pistil. Then, the pistil uses that pollen to create seeds for the plant! The bee picks up a little more pollen from this plant and flies off to a new plant. This is called pollination. Many insects like bees, butterflies, and more help to pollinate plants.

Would you like to see how pollination works? Let's do an activity!

Activity directions:

1. Draw a big flower on each piece of construction paper.

2. Lay the pieces out in a line and place a little flour in the center of the first flower.

3. Then, place a few Cheetos® in the center of the second flower.

4. Finally, place some cocoa powder in the center of the third flower.

Ask your student to put a glove on one hand. Then, pretend their hand is a bee and fly to the first flower. Direct them to land their hand on the flour and move their fingers around in it. Then, fly to the next flower and repeat, moving their fingers around on the Cheetos®.

Look at the Cheetos®. Do you see a little flour on them now? What about the glove? Do you see flour and Cheetos® powder?

Now, fly to the last flower and land in the cocoa powder. Do you see a little flour or Cheetos® powder in the cocoa now? What about on the glove?

Wow, that was really cool! That is how pollination works. The bee or other insect lands on a flower, and the pollen sticks to their fuzzy legs, just like it stuck to your fuzzy glove. Then, the bee or other insect flies to the next flower where it drops a little pollen from other flowers and picks up a little more pollen from the new flower, just like you picked up the powder from the flour and Cheetos®!

God made insects and flowers to work together. The bee receives nectar and pollinates the flower so that the flower can make seeds. God designed many things to work together, just like photosynthesis. People and animals breathe out carbon dioxide that plants need to absorb, and the plant creates oxygen that people and animals need to breathe. God designed many parts of creation to work together. Isn't that amazing?

Discussion Starters ▶

God designed many parts of creation to work together. Families need to work together, too.

Can you think of some ways you can help your family?

Can you describe how a bee or insect helps to pollinate a plant?

name

Share

What was your favorite thing you learned this week about flowers? [Allow student time to answer.] That is a really neat thing! Don't forget to share your favorite thing you learned about flowers and pollination with someone as you show them your page.

materials needed

☐ Pom poms
☐ Elmer's Glue®

This is a busy little bee! Let's pretend the pom-poms are pollen. Glue the pollen pom-poms to the legs of the bee. Once the glue is dry, add the page to your Science Notebook.

Blank for gluing page.

Seeds

3rd Day of Creation

week 17

Day 1

Learn

Are you ready for another science adventure this week as we explore creation? I know I am! Last week, we learned about flowers and pollination. After a flower is pollinated, do you remember what happens? The plant can make seeds. Let's talk about seeds this week!

God gave seeds a special job. Do you know what that is? [Allow student time to answer.] A seed's special job is to grow a brand new plant. There are many shapes and sizes of seeds. Some are very small while others are very large! Some seeds are deep inside the fruit of the plant. Can you think of any seeds that are like that? Apples, oranges, and peaches have seeds deep inside their fruit.

Other seeds are in a very hard shell, like the seeds of walnuts or acorns, and some seeds can be seen on the flower like those on a dandelion or a sunflower.

Sometimes, animals or people can eat seeds. Can you think of some seeds you might eat? We can eat the seeds in kiwi or pomegranates, or sometimes we eat whole seeds like walnuts, almonds, or peanuts. Some vegetables like peas are also seeds that we can eat.

Can you think of any other examples of seeds? [Allow student time to answer.] Dandelions have seeds that you can blow into the air. When the seed

Apple	✓
Cutting board	☐
Sharp knife — adult only!	☐

Weekly materials list

161

falls to the ground, it may start the process to grow a new dandelion plant. God made seeds very special. When it is warm enough, and there is water and fresh air for the seed, the plant inside the seed starts to grow. Have you ever watched a plant grow?

The seed may be on top of the dirt or underneath it, and you won't see very much happening at first. The seed has special food inside it to use while it grows. The seed will start to grow its roots, and the tiny plant will begin to grow. Soon, a tiny stem will begin to grow taller and taller. It may even have a tiny leaf or two. A new plant is growing! The new plant will grow taller and stronger, and eventually, it may also grow new seeds, too.

Did you know Jesus also told a story about seeds? Let's read that story in Matthew 13:1–9 (NIrV). Use your imagination to picture the farmer and the seeds as I read:

That same day Jesus left the house and sat by the Sea of Galilee. Large crowds gathered around him. So he got into a boat and sat down. All the people stood on the shore. Then he told them many things using stories. He said, "A farmer went out to plant his seed. He scattered the seed on the ground. Some fell on a path. Birds came and ate it up. Some seed fell on rocky places, where there wasn't much soil. The plants came up quickly, because the soil wasn't deep. When the sun came up, it burned the plants. They dried up because they had no roots. Other seed fell among thorns. The thorns grew up and crowded out the plants. Still other seed fell on good soil. It produced a crop 100, 60 or 30 times more than what was planted. Whoever has ears should listen."

Jesus said that hearing the message about His kingdom, about how He came to save us, is like the seed in this story. A seed needs to fall in good soil for it to grow, and it also needs strong roots, just like in Jesus' story. When we hear the message about Jesus and we understand it, we begin to grow in Him — just like the seed that fell on the good soil in Jesus' story.

Remember when we learned about roots and how we can also grow in our faith in Jesus? As we continue to grow, the roots of our faith grow stronger and stronger and we can also share about Jesus with our friends and family. What an amazing thing the seeds on a plant remind us of! Isn't it neat how studying science teaches us more about God?

Color the farmer.

name

The dandelion seed is blowing in the breeze. Help it get to the dirt so it can grow!

Discussion Starters

Search online for a time-lapse video of a seed growing, or even a full time-lapse from a seed to a flower. Be sure to preview the video first, then enjoy watching it with your student.

Can you think of ways you can begin to grow in your faith in Jesus?

Experience

materials needed
- ☐ Apple
- ☐ Cutting board
- ☐ Sharp knife — adult only!

We're learning about seeds this week. Let's take a deeper look inside seeds. [Hold apple up.] This is an apple. In the spring, the apple tree grows beautiful little flowers. We call them apple blossoms. Those apple blossoms attract bees, insects, and butterflies. Do you remember what they do? [Allow student to answer.]

The insects pollinate the flowers! Once the flowers are pollinated, the tree begins to grow the seeds. For an apple tree, the seeds grow inside the fruit — the apple. Apples have seeds inside them. How many seeds do you think are inside this apple? Let's cut it open and find out!

Teacher, carefully cut open the apple and locate all of the seeds. Count them and set aside.

How many seeds did we find inside the apple? [Allow student to answer.] Let's look a little closer at these seeds.

Teacher, carefully cut one of the seeds in half if one was not already cut while slicing the apple.

On the outside of the seed, we see a thin dark layer — this is called the seed coat. The seed coat helps to protect the seed until it is just right for the seed to start growing. At one tip of the seed is the radicle, but it may be a bit hard to see. When the seed is ready to grow, this part will grow down into the dirt to begin forming roots for the plant.

There is a lot of white inside the seed, isn't there? The middle part of the seed is called the cotyledon (pronounced kaa-tuh-lee-dn). The cotyledon stores food for the plant and will grow into the first leaves of the plant. Wow, there is a lot in the inside of an apple seed!

This is what the inside of an apple looks like:

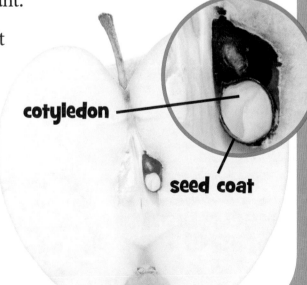

cotyledon

seed coat

name

Can you draw a picture of the apple below? Don't forget the seeds!

Discussion Starters ►

What kinds of seeds can you find outside?

Can you find any seeds on dried plants, nuts, or fruits?

The next time you eat a meal, see if you are eating any seeds.

Day

Share

name

Wow, seeds are sure a special part of God's creation! I'm ready to add a new page to our Science Notebook. How about you? Let's get started! Color the pictures of the seed growing tall and strong. Don't forget to share what you've learned this week with someone else. Be sure to tell them that seeds remind us to continue growing in our love for Jesus.

Trace the words "I can grow in Jesus."

Trace the picture.

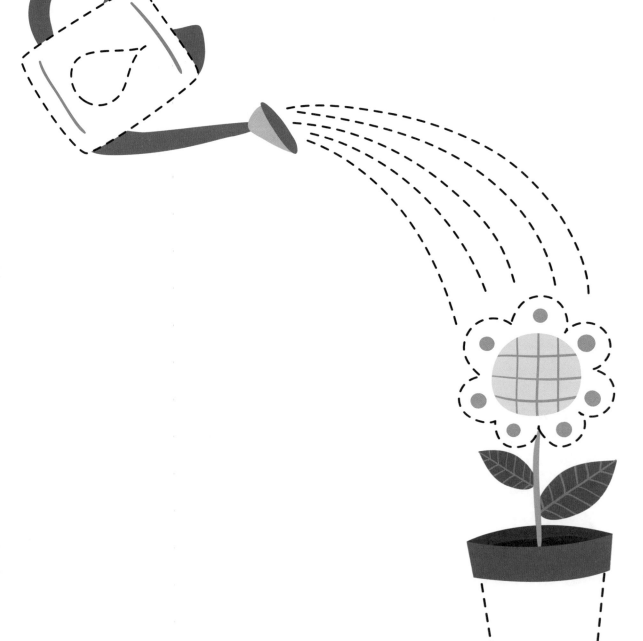

The Fourth Day of Creation

week 18

4th Day of Creation

Day

Learn

Welcome back to a new science adventure as we study God's creation! It's time to explore the fourth day of creation. Are you excited? So far, we've learned about the first, second, and third days of creation. Do you remember what God made on the first day of creation?

God made the heavens, earth, and light on the first day of creation! What about the second day, do you remember? God made the atmosphere — the sky — on the second day of creation. We've also learned about the third day of creation during the last few weeks. Do you remember what God made on the third day of creation?

God made dry ground and plants on the third day of creation. We learned about continents and the layers inside the earth. We also learned some amazing things about plants as we studied leaves and photosynthesis, pollination, and seeds. What was your favorite part?

I wonder what God made on the fourth day of creation . . . do you wonder, too? Where do you think we should look for our answers? In the Bible! Let's read from Genesis 1:14–19 (NIrV):

God said, "Let there be lights in the huge space of the sky. Let them separate the day from the

Paper plate	✓
Red, orange, and yellow tissue paper or construction paper	☐
Glue stick	☐

Weekly materials list

169

night. Let the lights set the times for the holy celebrations and the days and the years. Let them be lights in the huge space of the sky to give light on the earth." And that's exactly what happened. God made two great lights. He made the larger light to rule over the day and the smaller light to rule over the night. He also made the stars. God put the lights in the huge space of the sky to give light on the earth. He put them there to rule over the day and the night. He put them there to separate light from darkness. God saw that it was good. There was evening, and there was morning. It was day four.

I think we heard our answer. Did you hear it, too? God made the sun, moon, and stars on the fourth day of creation. Ooh, I'm so excited to study the sun, moon, and stars! I wonder if Cain and Abel ever asked Adam and Eve about the fourth day of creation? In our last story, Adam, Eve, Cain, and Abel were walking and talking about flowers. Let's imagine what happened next!

Cain and Abel had learned a lot about flowers during their walk, and they enjoyed looking at and smelling many different kinds of flowers. Later that night, Abel started to wonder what God had made on the fourth day of creation. He decided he would ask his mom and dad the next morning during breakfast. He prayed and thanked God for the beautiful flowers, and then he fell asleep.

The sun rose the next morning, and a rooster crowed far away. Abel jumped out of bed. He couldn't wait to hear what God had made on the fourth day of creation. "Mom! Dad!" Abel called through their tent. He found Eve and gave her a good morning hug. "Mom, what did God make on the fourth day of creation?"

"Good morning, Abel. That's a good question. Let's eat breakfast, then we will talk about the fourth day of creation." Adam and Cain woke up and they all ate breakfast together.

Abel used a cloth to wipe his mouth after breakfast, then exclaimed, "Okay! What did God make on the fourth day of creation?" Adam and Eve laughed. They were happy Abel was excited to learn.

"On the fourth day of creation, God made the sun, moon, and stars, Abel," Eve replied as Abel clapped his hands.

"I can't wait to learn about the sun, moon, and stars, Mom!" he said.

"I asked God about the fourth day of creation, too, Abel," Adam said. "The sun is a large star and God put it at just the perfect distance from the earth. The sun gives us light during the day, and it gives us heat to make the earth not too hot and not too cold for us to live on."

"Wow! It sure is amazing that God put everything in creation right in the perfect place," Abel replied.

"Yes, it is, buddy! Let's get started on the day now, and we'll talk more as we get to work." Abel helped to clean up after breakfast. He was excited to work with his dad and learn more about the sun, moon, and stars.

The sun is the larger light God made to rule the day. The sun is very, very big. We could fit one million of our planet earths inside of it! That is bigger than I can imagine. But, even though the sun is that big, the sun is just a medium-sized star. That means God also created stars far bigger than the sun.

Sometimes, when we study God's creation, we learn about something amazing — like the sun — and it reminds us that God is great, wise, and powerful. As we learn about the sun, moon, and stars, the amazing design God gave them reminds us to praise and worship Him. Psalm 113:2–3 (NIrV) says, *"Let us praise the name of the LORD, both now and forever. From the sunrise in the east to the sunset in the west, may the name of the LORD be praised."*

We're going to continue learning about the sun as we study the fourth day of creation. As we learn, don't forget to praise God and thank Him for His amazing design!

name

Trace the words "sun," "moon," and "stars" below each image. God made the sun, moon, and stars on the fourth day of creation!

sun

moon

stars

 **Let's memorize**

Psalm 113:2–3 (NIrV)

" Let us **praise** the name of the **LORD**, both now and forever. From the sunrise in the east to the sunset in the west, may the name of the **LORD** be **praised**. "

	Actions
praise • praised	Place your hands together as if in prayer or raise them in worship.
LORD	Make an L with your pointer finger and thumb on your left hand. Place your left hand at your right shoulder and cross it in front of you to your left hip — almost like you are wearing a sash and tracing over it with your hand. You can also search for this sign online to see it in action by searching "sign language for Lord."
sunrise in the east to the sunset in the west	Point your finger toward your left side then trace it up and over your head to your right side, like you are tracing the path of the sun through the sky.

Experience

materials needed

- [ ] Paper plate
- [ ] Glue stick
- [ ] Red, orange, and yellow tissue paper or construction paper, cut or torn into approximately 1-inch pieces

Are you ready to learn more about the sun? In our last lesson, we learned that God made the sun, moon, and stars on the fourth day of creation. We also learned a little about the sun! The sun is very, very large. Do you remember how many earths could fit inside? One million! We also learned that the sun is a medium-sized star. There are much bigger stars.

The sun gives us light and keeps the earth at the perfect temperature for us to live. The sun looks big in the sky because it is the star closest to earth at about 93 million miles away. Even though the sun is the closest star to earth, it is still very, very far away.

God placed the sun at the perfect distance, not too far away from the earth — this would make the earth too cold. The sun is also not too close to the earth — this would make the earth too hot. Remember when we learned about light and how light travels so fast? The sun is far away from us, and light travels very fast. As light travels from the sun, it takes about 8 minutes for that light from the sun to reach us here on earth. How amazing!

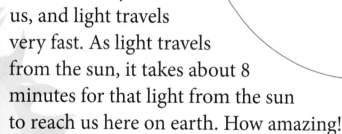

If the sun were as tall as a typical front door, Earth would be about the size of a nickel.

The sun is made mostly of two elements called helium and hydrogen, and the surface of the sun is about 11,000 degrees Fahrenheit. Put your hand on my forehead. Can you feel how hot I am? You and I are about 98.5 degrees Fahrenheit. That means the sun is over 100 times warmer than we are. The sun provides the perfect amount of heat to keep the earth at just the right temperature for us to live. The sun gives us light and heat so that we can live on the earth.

The sun looks like a big, fiery, burning ball with areas of red, orange, and yellow. Let's make our own example of the sun!

Activity directions:

Glue pieces of construction paper or tissue paper onto the paper plate to resemble the sun.

Teacher tip: Save the paper plate sun from our lesson today for next week—it will be part of next week's activity day.

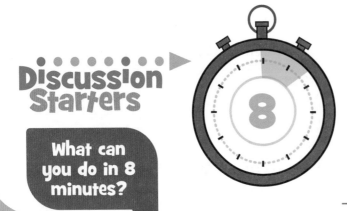

Discussion Starters

What can you do in 8 minutes?

Set a timer for 8 minutes to see how long it takes light to travel 93 million miles from the sun to earth. When you set the timer, ask your student to imagine light leaving the sun and traveling through space. When the timer beeps, remind your student that the light made its way all the way from the sun to us — light travels a long way very quickly!

name

We've learned a lot about the fourth day of creation and the sun this week. Did you have fun? You know what today is — it's time to add a new page to our Science Notebook! We've been learning about the fourth day of creation when God made the sun, moon, and stars. We've learned a little about the sun this week. Do you remember what the sun gives us? Light and heat!

Color the pictures of the earth and the sun and write "The sun gives us light and heat." Then, add this page to your Science Notebook. Don't forget to tell someone that God created the sun, and He put it in the perfect spot to give us the light and heat we need.

Trace the text and color the sun.

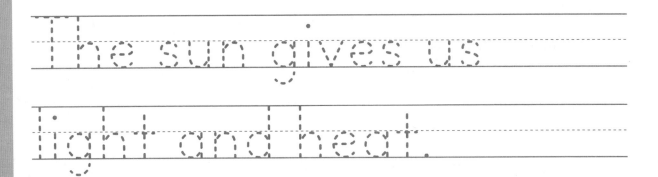

The sun gives us light and heat.

Sun

4th Day of Creation

Day

Learn Are you ready to continue exploring the fourth day of creation? I know I am! First, let's stand up and jump as high as we can. Ready, set, go!

What happens when you jump? Are you able to stay in the air or do you fall back down to the ground? When you jump as high as you can, you still come back down to the ground. This is because of gravity. What is gravity? Well, gravity is the force that keeps us here on earth. Gravity is created by really large objects — like the earth or the sun — and it pulls other objects toward them.

The earth's gravity pulls us toward the ground. It's what keeps us safe and sound on the ground instead of floating away into the sky. The earth's gravity also pulls on the moon, and it keeps the moon traveling around and around and around the earth. When the gravity from something big pulls on a smaller object and keeps it traveling in a circle, we call this an orbit.

The sun has gravity, too, and it pulls on objects and keeps them rotating around it as well. The sun's gravity pulls the earth in an orbit around it. The earth travels in a big circle around the sun. It takes 365 days for the earth to travel all the way around the sun.

Paper plate sun from week 18	✓
String or yarn, 4–5 feet long	☐
Elmer's glue®	☐

Weekly materials list

Let's read Genesis 1:14 (NIrV) again: *"God said, 'Let there be lights in the huge space of the sky. Let them separate the day from the night. Let the lights set the times for the holy celebrations and the days and the years.' "*

A year is one way we measure time. A year has 365 days — the same amount of time it takes the earth to travel all the way around the sun. Each year, we make one full trip around the sun. The sun and the moon help us keep track of and measure time, just like God said.

The earth is called a planet in outer space, and there are other planets that orbit around the sun as well. The names of those planets are Mercury, Venus, Mars, Jupiter, Saturn, Uranus, and Neptune. Pluto also orbits around the sun, but it is not a planet like the others. We call Pluto a dwarf-planet, and we've found five moons that orbit it. Each planet is different and beautiful, but only the planet Earth is specially designed for us to be able to live on.

Each of the other planets and the earth travel around the sun in an orbit. Some travel very close to the sun, and others orbit the sun very far away. The gravity of the sun keeps each one in place.

name

Let's trace the orbit of each planet!

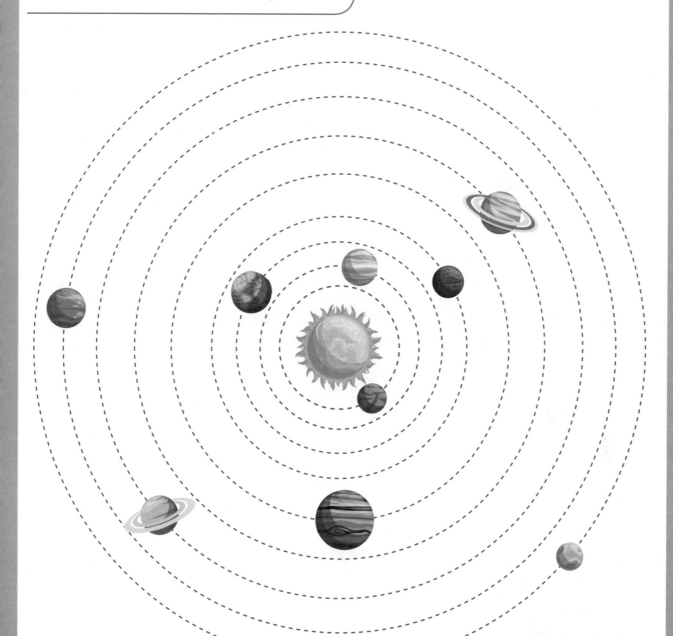

Discussion Starters

Gather various objects — some light, some heavier. Throw or drop them and watch what happens.

Do the objects all fall back to the ground — even the lightest objects?

This is gravity in action!

How old are you?

How many trips around the sun have you made?

Experience

materials needed

- [ ] Paper plate sun from week 18
- [ ] String or yarn, 4–5 feet long

It sure was neat learning about gravity and the orbit of the earth and other planets around the sun in our last lesson! Today, let's make our own orbit — are you ready? Well, then what are we waiting for? Let's get started!

I'm going to pretend to be the sun and hold one end of a big piece of string. You will pretend to be a planet and you'll hold the other end of the string. When you start walking, what do you think will happen? Will you be able to walk anywhere you want, or only as far as the string will let you?

You think you'll be able to _____ .

[fill in with student's answer]

Do you remember what this is called? This is your hypothesis — what you think will happen. Let's see what happens!

Activity directions:

Teacher tip: This activity may also be completed outside if you need a little more space or would like to create a larger orbit.

1. Teacher, hold the paper plate sun from Week 18's activity — you are pretending to be the sun.

2. Hold one end of the string or yarn and instruct your student to hold the other end. The string is your pretend "gravity."

3. Instruct your student to walk out as far as the string will let them and begin to walk around you but hold onto the string.

As they walk, point out how the string keeps them traveling at a certain distance around you. This is like the gravity of the sun, which keeps the planets traveling at a certain distance around it as well. Ask your student to walk or run a little faster. Does the gravity of the string still keep them traveling the same path? Switch places and let your student be the sun and rotate around your student.

That was fun! We made our own orbit. The string was like the gravity of the sun, and it kept you and me rotating around right where we were supposed to be. When you held the string, were you able to travel anywhere you wanted to or only as far as the string let you? Was this what you thought would happen?

The gravity of the sun is just like the string. It pulls on the planets and keeps them traveling around in just the right place. Gravity is a pretty cool part of God's creation, isn't it? Gravity keeps our feet on the earth, and it keeps the earth rotating around the sun in just the right place. Thank you, God, for gravity!

Image Credit: NASA

Discussion Starters

Your student may enjoy repeating this activity with a friend or family member. Ask them to explain gravity and orbits as they do it. Read *When You See a Star,* also available from Master Books®.

Can you tell me what gravity does?

What is an orbit?

Gravity keeps our feet on the earth. Can you imagine what it would be like if the earth didn't have the perfect amount of gravity? What if there wasn't enough gravity? What do you think that would be like?

Draw a picture of what you think it would look like on the earth without gravity.

name

It was so much fun to continue exploring the sun, gravity, and orbits this week! Can you guess what day it is? It's the day we add a new page to our Science Notebook! Woohoo!

The sun's gravity pulls on the earth and keeps the earth traveling around the sun in an orbit, just like the string in our activity kept us traveling around in a circle. Let's glue a piece of string between the earth and the sun to remind us that the sun's gravity keeps the earth orbiting around it. Once the glue dries, add this page to your Science Notebook and don't forget to tell someone about gravity and orbits!

Blank for gluing.

Moon — Surface

4th Day of Creation

Day

Learn

Are you ready to start another science adventure? Close your eyes . . . let's use our imagination and pretend it is night. It is dark outside. Do you hear the crickets chirping? What might you see in the sky on a dark night? [Allow student to answer.] The moon and stars!

You can open your eyes now. This week, we are going to explore the moon! We learned about gravity last week. The earth's gravity is what keeps us on the ground. Just like the sun's gravity keeps the earth orbiting around the sun, the earth's gravity pulls on the moon and keeps it orbiting around the earth.

Flour or playdough	✓
Container	
Small objects such as pebbles or marbles	
White paint	
Black construction paper	
Cotton ball	
Pencil	
Optional: Clothespin	
Hole punch	

Sometimes the moon is closer to the earth, and sometimes it is a little farther away, but the moon is 238,712 miles away from the earth on average. That is so far away! But remember, the sun is much, much farther away from us than that.

The moon is very big, but not as big as the earth. The moon is about one-fourth the size of the earth. That means if we could split the earth into four big pieces, the moon would be about as big as one of those pieces of the earth.

Weekly materials list

187

I wonder . . . do you think Cain and Abel ever asked Adam and Eve about the moon? Let's imagine they did! In our last story, Abel had learned what God made on the fourth day of creation. He was excited to start working with Adam and learn more about the sun. Let's imagine what happened next!

Imagine That!
Bible-inspired stories

Abel had worked hard with his Dad all day, and they had talked a lot about the sun. Abel had learned that the sun is a star and that it has gravity that keeps the earth rotating around it in an orbit. The day went on, and finally the sun had gone down. Nighttime had begun. The crickets were singing their songs now. Their "chirp, chirp" could be heard all around the tent. In the sky, there were no clouds, and the moon was full and bright.

Adam, Eve, Cain, and Abel were inside their tent. They had eaten dinner and cleaned things up. Now Adam was tickling the boys. They were all laughing hard. "Dad, Dad, Dad!" Abel exclaimed through giggles. "Please . . . stop . . . tickling!" Adam chuckled as he stopped tickling and wrapped Abel in a big hug.

Cain glanced at the tent door where soft moonlight was coming in. "Dad, the moon is really bright tonight. I can see the light in the door. Can we go outside and look at it?" Cain asked.

"Of course!" Adam and Eve replied. They all walked outside and sat in the soft grass as they looked up at the moon.

The moon's soft glow was beautiful. "Dad, how does the moon make light?" asked Cain.

"That is a good question. I asked God that same question one night," replied Adam. Adam thought back to that night when He had asked God how the moon makes light.

"Actually, the moon doesn't make its own light, Cain. I was amazed when I learned that! God made the moon to reflect the light from the sun. The moon reflects the light from the sun to give us a soft glow at night."

"Whoa, I didn't know that!" said Abel.

Cain thought quietly then asked, "So, what keeps the moon near the earth? Is that gravity again?"

"Yes, it is, Cain," Eve said. "The earth has gravity, too, and it pulls the moon and keeps it orbiting around the earth. God's design in creation is amazing. When the sun comes up in the morning and goes down at night, it reminds me that God is faithful even when I am not." Eve looked down sadly. "God made creation perfect, boys, but Dad and I chose to not listen to His directions."

Eve wiped a tear from her eye as Adam said, "Our sin broke His creation, and now things aren't perfect anymore. I'll never forget feeling afraid for the first time as God walked through the Garden after we made the wrong choice. I had been able to walk and talk with God, and I had never felt afraid before! This time, I was scared, and I hid from God."

"There were consequences for our sin, boys. That means when we made our choice, other things that we didn't mean to happen happened. We felt sad, afraid, and ashamed, and we couldn't walk and talk closely with God anymore because He is holy and sinless," Eve explained softly.

"I miss walking and talking closely with God," she said as she wiped another tear.

Adam held her hand. "I do, too," he said. "Boys, we all have choices to make. You will make choices throughout your whole lives. We can live our lives as God tells us to, or we can go our own way."

Adam thought back to the Garden of Eden where he was able to walk and talk with God, where he didn't feel afraid or alone. He wished he could go back and make a different choice. "It's always better to follow God's way, Cain and Abel. He knows far better than we do. He is faithful, and He loves us. His ways and directions protect us."

They all sat together quietly thinking about what Adam and Eve had said as they looked at the soft glow of the moon. It was getting a little colder, and Cain started to shiver. "Let's go inside now and get ready for bed." Adam sighed as he stood up, then they all made their way back inside.

I'm so glad God had a plan to save us from our sins, aren't you? John 3:16 says, *"For God so loved the world that he gave his one and only Son, that whoever believes in him shall not perish but have eternal life."* God sent Jesus to save us from our sins so that we can have a relationship with God. Even though our sin broke the world, I'm so glad God is faithful to us and that He loves us so much.

The moon reminds us that God is faithful. The moon reflects the light of the sun, and that reflection creates the soft glow we see on a dark night. We're going to learn more about the moon in our next few lessons, but for now, let's color the night sky and trace John 3:16!

name

Trace John 3:16.

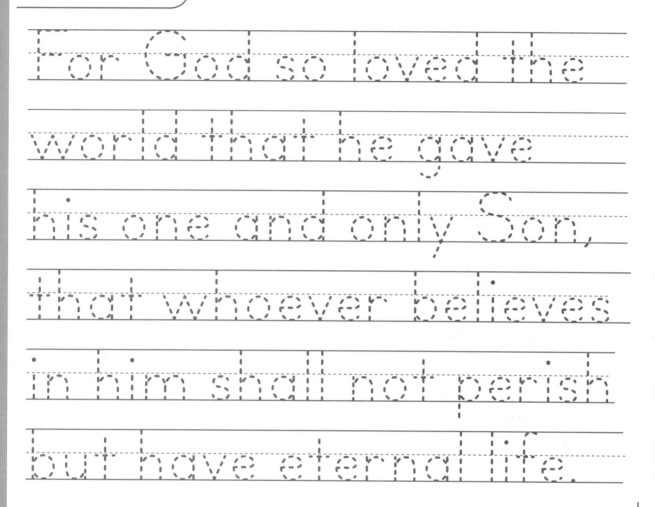

For God so loved the
world that he gave
his one and only Son,
that whoever believes
in him shall not perish
but have eternal life.

Discussion Starters ▶ Teacher, cut a round fruit or vegetable into four pieces. Compare and contrast the size of the fruit or vegetable to the size of just one-fourth with your student. This is like the size difference between the earth and the moon. Or, make five balls of playdough of the same size. Squish four of the balls together into one big ball. Compare the size of the large ball and the small ball.

Sin separates us from God, and it has sad consequences. The price of sin is death. Our sin broke the world, but the story isn't finished yet! God sent Jesus Christ to pay the price of our sin so that we can have a relationship with God. Someday, Jesus will also come back to earth, and He will make everything right again.

Color your voyage into space.

Experience

materials needed

☐ Flour or playdough

☐ Container

☐ Small objects such as pebbles or marbles to drop into the flour or playdough

We're learning about the moon this week. Would you like to learn a little more about the surface of the moon? Me too! When we look at the moon at night, we see dark areas on the surface, as well as lighter areas.

The dark areas are called maria. These areas are large areas that are covered in lava — like what comes out of a volcano — that has hardened. The hardened lava is darker than the rest of the moon.

There are also craters on the moon. Craters are formed when something crashes into the moon. The moon doesn't have an atmosphere to protect it like the earth does, so sometimes an asteroid or meteor — big pieces of rock in outer space — fall into the moon and hit the surface very hard. We're going to make our own craters in just a little bit, but first, let's keep talking about the surface of the moon.

Put your hands together in the shape of a cup, as if you were going to hold water in them — this is kind of like a crater. The crater has a deep center, like the center of your hands, and it also has walls that are tall above the deep center like the top edge of your hands. Some areas of the crater may be much taller above the deep center,

and these look like mountains. The mountains on the moon are made from the edges of craters. The tallest mountain is about three miles tall. Are you ready to make some craters of your own? Let's get started!

Activity directions:

Option A-Flour	Option B-Playdough
1. Spread flour flat about 1–2 inches in a container.	1. Shape playdough into a round ball and place it into a container.
2. Instruct student to drop a small object, pebble, or marble into the container of flour. The object will create a small crater. Pull the object out of the crater and look at the imprint.	2. Instruct the student to drop a small object, pebble, or marble onto the ball of playdough. Depending on the weight of the object, the student may need to drop it from a little higher in order to create an impression in the ball.
3. Continue to drop a small object, pebble, or marble into the container until there are several imprints in the flour.	3. Rotate the ball of playdough and continue to drop a small object, pebble, or marble onto it.
	4. Pick up the ball of playdough and observe the surface.

What do you see?

Can you describe the craters?

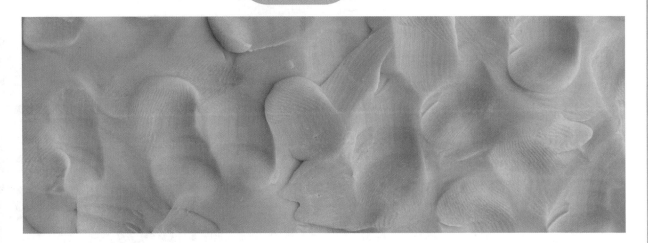

Discussion Starters

What are maria?

Did you see the deep centers in the craters you made?

Did the edge of any of your craters look like a mountain?

Share

materials needed

☐ White paint

☐ Black construction paper

☐ Cotton ball

☐ Pencil

☐ Optional: Clothespin for less mess. Use the clothespin to hold the cotton ball, and the student can hold onto the top of the clothespin.

☐ Hole punch

name

We've learned so much about the moon already, and it's time to add a new page to our Science Notebook! First, draw a big circle with the pencil on the black piece of paper. It will be a bit hard to see on the paper, but that's okay! This is our outline for the moon.

Next, dip the cotton ball into the white paint and begin to paint inside the circle of the moon on the black paper. To paint it, first press the cotton ball onto the paper and then pick it back up. Repeat. Be sure to leave dark areas on the moon, too — these will be our maria!

Once the page is dry, ask your parent to add it to your Science Notebook Be sure to tell someone else what you learned about the moon this week!

Help the astronaut get to the moon!

Moon — Phases

4th Day of Creation

Learn We've been learning about the fourth day of creation, and we've learned some really neat things about the sun and moon in the last few weeks! Have you ever looked up at the moon at night and noticed that sometimes the moon is full and round, sometimes it looks like a half moon, and other nights the moon is a crescent shape — like a banana?

I'd like to learn why the moon looks different — how about you? Let's talk about the moon! The moon orbits the earth. That means it is traveling around and around the earth — just like the earth orbits the sun. As the moon orbits the earth, it is also spinning at just the right speed so that we always see the same side of the moon. Isn't that really neat?

The moon reflects light from the sun. As it orbits, the moon looks like it changes shapes from full to half to crescent because the amount of light we can see reflected changes as it orbits. The moon changes appearance in a regular pattern or cycle of 29½ days. That means we know what the moon will look like ahead of time because God made it to follow that pattern.

Let's learn about the cycle, or phases, of the moon! The first phase is called the new moon, but we actually don't see the moon during this phase because the sunlight is shining on the far side of the moon that we can't see. Because the sunlight is shining on the back of the moon, there

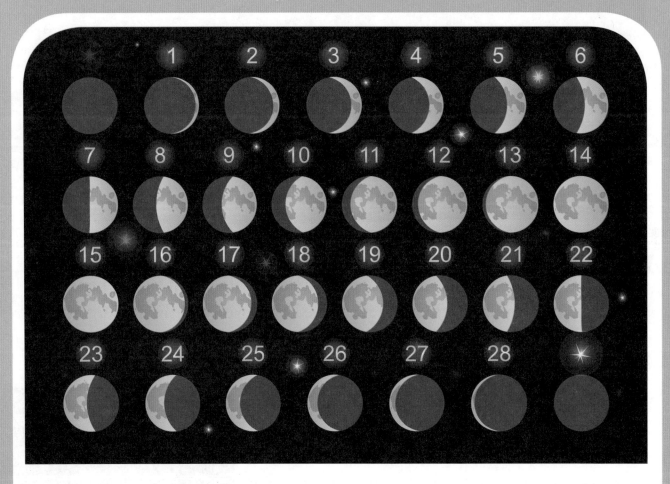

is no light reflected on the front side of the moon we can see. So, we don't see the moon in the sky. When we don't see the moon, we call this the new moon.

As the moon continues to orbit, suddenly we'll see a very small crescent of the moon appear. It looks like a sliver of the moon, shaped like a banana. The crescent will grow a little bigger each night as the moon orbits and we see more and more sunlight reflected. We call this "waxing crescent."

The crescent of the moon grows a little bigger every night until it looks less like a crescent shape and more like half of the moon. When we see half of the moon, this is called the first quarter moon. Each night, we continue to see more and more of the moon — now it is more than half! When we see more than half of the moon, we say it is "waxing gibbous." "Gibbous" is a fancy word

Option A:
Oreos™ ✓
Option B:
Flashlight ☐
Ball, such as a
tennis or soccer ball ☐

that means we see more than half of the moon, but not the full moon yet.

Then, one night we'll see the full moon and we call this the full moon phase. The moon continues to orbit, and it will begin to disappear again little by little. We call this "waning gibbous." Waning is a word that means the moon is getting smaller. Soon, we will see just half of the moon again. This is called the third quarter. Then the crescent shape appears once more when the moon looks like a banana. This is called "waning crescent." The crescent will become thinner and thinner until the moon disappears and we are back at the new moon phase.

Then, the moon will repeat this pattern all over again. We call this pattern the moon phases, or lunar phases. God designed the earth, moon, and sun, and He made them to follow patterns so perfectly that we can even know what the moon will look like ahead of time. Isn't that amazing?

Just as the moon is faithful to follow this pattern, God is also faithful. He is who He says He is, and He does what He says He will do. First John 1:9 (NIrV) reminds us, *"But God is faithful and fair. If we confess our sins, he will forgive our sins. He will forgive every wrong thing we have done. He will make us pure."*

I'm so glad God is faithful to forgive our sins when we tell Him we are sorry, aren't you? When you see the moon follow its pattern in the sky, be sure to remember that God is faithful, too.

| Waxing crescent | First quarter | Waxing gibbous | Full moon | Waning gibbous | Third quarter | Waning crescent |

MOON PHASES

The moon follows a pattern. Let's trace the name of each phase. Ask your parent to read the name as you trace it.

new moon

waxing crescent

first quarter

waxing gibbous

full moon

waning gibbous

third quarter

waning crescent

Discussion Starters

Go outside on a clear night.

What phase is the moon in tonight?

Moon Phases Calendar

Fill in the circles to show how the moon looks each night.

Sunday	Monday	Tuesday	Wednesday	Thursday	Friday	Saturday
◯	◯	◯	◯	◯	◯	◯
◯	◯	◯	◯	◯	◯	◯
◯	◯	◯	◯	◯	◯	◯
◯	◯	◯	◯	◯	◯	◯

Day

We've been learning about the phases of the moon this week. Are you ready to learn a little more about moon phases? Let's start our activity!

Experience

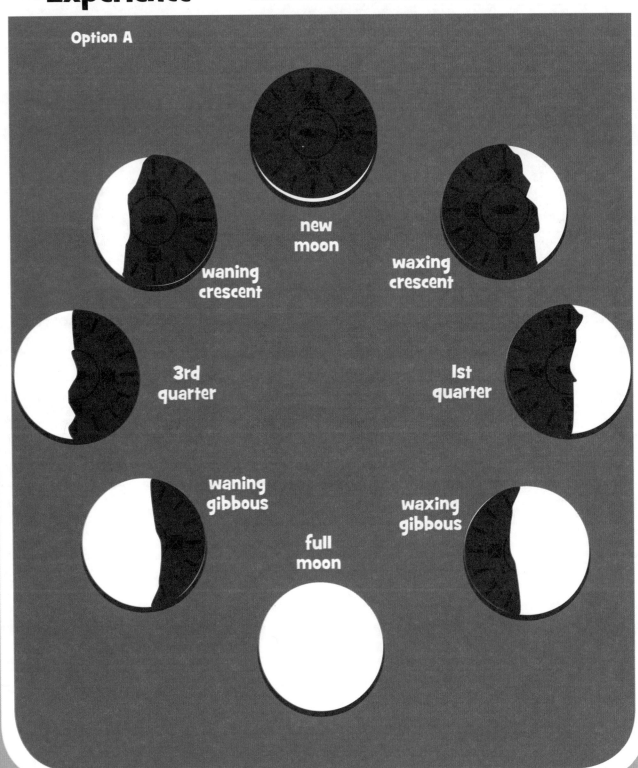

Option A

new moon

waning crescent

waxing crescent

3rd quarter

1st quarter

waning gibbous

waxing gibbous

full moon

Option A

1. Split 8 Oreos™ apart so that the frosting is on one side of the cookie.

2. At the top of the manipulative sheet, place one cookie half that does not have frosting on it. This represents the new moon.

3. Remove frosting from the next Oreo™ to create a crescent of frosting on the right side. Place this cookie in the next circle to the right of the new moon, this represents the waxing crescent moon.

4. Remove half of the frosting from the next cookie and place it in the next circle. This represents the first quarter moon.

5. Remove a small crescent of frosting on the left side of the next cookie to represent the waxing gibbous phase and place it in the next circle.

6. Place a cookie with all of the frosting on the next circle to represent the full moon.

7. Remove a small crescent of frosting from the right side of the next cookie to represent the waning gibbous moon and place in the next circle.

8. Remove half of the frosting from the right side of the next cookie to represent the third quarter moon.

9. Remove all but a sliver of frosting on the left side of the final cookie to finish the moon phases with waning crescent.

10. Eat a few (or all!) of the phases of the moon!

Option B

1. Dim the lights (or go into a dark room) and ask your student to hold the flashlight.

2. Slowly move the ball into the beam of light from the flashlight and observe how the light illuminates the ball. First partially, then half, then whole, then partially, and then none.

3. Explain how this is similar to the moon. As the moon orbits, the amount of sunlight reflected to earth changes — just like the amount of light on the ball changed. This creates the shapes of the moon that we see.

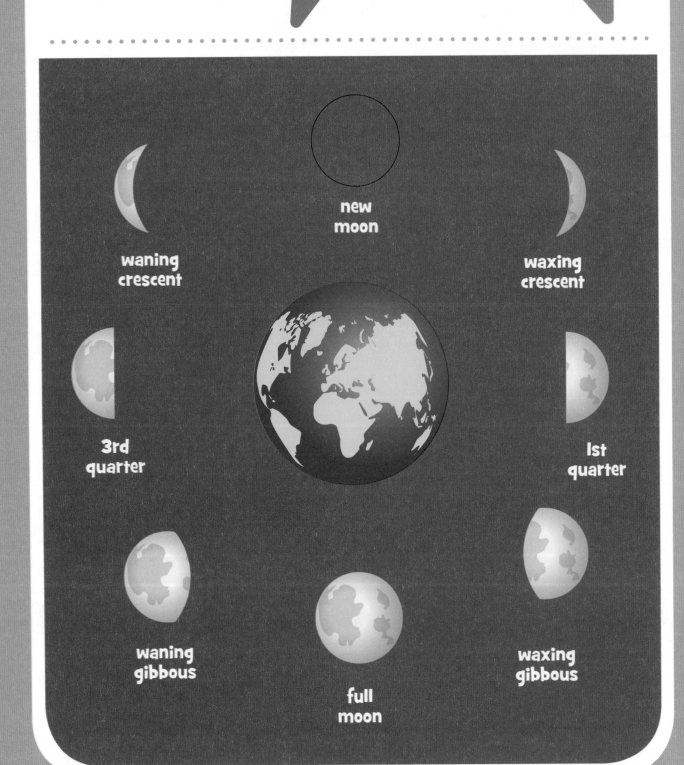

Share

name

We've been learning about the phases of the moon this week, and it's been a lot of fun! Are you ready to tell someone else about what we've been learning? Let's add a new page to your Science Notebook!

Color in the circle to show what the moon looks like in each phase. If you need help remembering, look at the picture on the previous page.

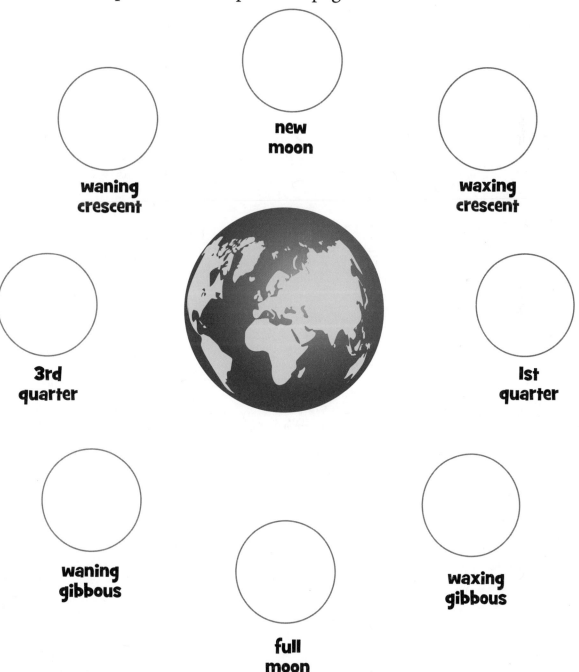

new
moon

waning
crescent

waxing
crescent

3rd
quarter

1st
quarter

waning
gibbous

waxing
gibbous

full
moon

Did you know that people have traveled to the moon in spaceships? We call them astronauts. What do you think it would be like to be an astronaut?

Can you draw a picture of your spaceship?

Stars

4th Day of Creation

Day

Learn

Close your eyes, and let's imagine it's dark outside! It's nighttime. There is a cool breeze blowing across your face, and crickets are chirping in the background — chirp, chirp, chirp. If you look up to the sky during the night, what might you see? Stars! Lots and lots of stars. Open your eyes back up. Are you ready for another science adventure? Let's talk about stars!

We've already learned some about the star that is closest to us. Do you remember what that is? The sun! The sun is a star, and it is the closest star to earth. The sun is about 93 million miles away from the earth. That is a huge number! The stars we see in the night sky are much, much farther away from earth than the sun. That is why they look so much smaller.

There are more stars than we can count in the sky. Some are much, much bigger than the sun, and some are smaller. Stars burn gases, and some stars burn hotter than others. The color of a star depends on how hot the star burns. Stars that don't burn quite as hot look red to us, while the stars that burn the hottest look blue or white in the sky. Some stars, like the sun, look yellow because they don't burn the hottest like blue or white stars, but they don't have the coolest temperature like a red star either. These stars have a temperature in-between the hottest and the coolest, so we see them as yellow.

Do you remember when we studied light, and we saw how fast light travels? When we study the universe, we measure how far things are from us using light. Light travels super fast. In one year — the time from your 5th birthday to the time of your 6th birthday, for example — light travels 6 trillion miles. What a huge number! I can't even imagine that distance. Scientists call this a light-year. A light-year is the distance light travels in one year, and it's a long, long way.

Alpha Centauri A and B

European Space Agency/NASA

The Alpha Centauri star system is the closest star system to the earth. There are three stars in this system. The first star is called Alpha Centauri A. This star is larger than the sun. The second star is called Alpha Centauri B, and it is smaller and not as hot as Alpha Centauri A. The third star is called Alpha Centauri C, or Proxima Centauri.

The Alpha Centauri star system is over 4 light-years away from earth. That means if we could shine a flashlight from earth toward the Alpha Centauri system, it would take that light — which travels so fast — more than 4 years to reach the stars! Wow!

So, how old are you now? [Allow student to answer.] Let's add four. How old would you be when the light reached the Alpha Centauri star system? The universe that God made is incredibly big, and there are millions and millions of stars in the sky — more than we can even count.

Do you think Adam, Eve, Cain, and Abel ever talked about the stars in the sky? In our last story, they were talking about the moon. Let's imagine what happened next!

6 popsicle sticks	✓
Glue	☐
String or yarn	☐
Optional: Silver or gold glitter	☐

Weekly materials list

Imagine That!

Bible-inspired stories

Adam, Eve, Cain, and Abel had finished talking about the moon when Abel noticed all of the tiny spots of light in the sky. Hundreds and thousands of tiny lights were scattered over the dark night sky. "Dad, what are those tiny lights in the sky? There are so many tiny spots of light!"

"Well, those are called stars, Abel. God made the sun, moon, and stars on the fourth day of creation. There are more stars in the sky than we can count, but God knows just how many there are. The sun is a star. It is closer to earth than all of the other stars. That is why the sun is big, but the stars we see at night are very small spots of light in the sky because they are farther away from us."

"Wow! Let's see how many we can count!" Abel exclaimed.

Cain looked toward the sky. "I like to connect the stars with my imagination to make pictures in the sky."

"That sounds like fun, Cain! Count the stars with me, and then we'll make pictures!" Abel replied as they all began to count the stars.

· ·

When we look at the night sky and see all the stars, so many more than we can count, they remind us that God is great. God made all of the stars, and He knows each one of them. Genesis 1:16 says, *"God made two great lights — the greater light to govern the day and the lesser light to govern the night. He also made the stars."*

name

Count the stars, then color some red, some blue, and some yellow. Then, trace the words "God made the stars."

How many stars?

God made the stars.

Discussion Starters

How long is one mile?

How long does it take you to go 1 mile, 5 miles, or 10 miles?

- Get in the car and go for a quick drive. Explain that these are incredibly small distances compared to the distances we measure in the universe.

- Family activity: Watch *Created Cosmos* available through Master Books or Answers in Genesis. *Created Cosmos* reveals the incredible scope and scale of the universe. The material will be advanced for young students; however, your student may also enjoy seeing the scale and beauty of the universe.

Experience

materials needed

- ☐ 6 popsicle sticks
- ☐ Glue
- ☐ String or yarn
- ☐ Optional: Silver or gold glitter

We're learning about stars this week! Today, we're going to make a pretend star out of popsicle sticks.

Activity directions:

Teacher tip: Allow the student to position the sticks a couple of times before they glue them together to make sure they are understanding the activity directions.

1. Glue the first 3 popsicle sticks together into a triangle shape. Then, glue the next 3 popsicle sticks into a triangle.

2. Place one triangle on the table, then rotate the other triangle so the points alternate like so:

3. Glue the two triangles together.

4. Spread glue on the top of the star and sprinkle glitter across the top. Allow to dry.

5. Once dried, attach the string to the star and hang.

Your star looks beautiful!

Discussion Starters

Go outside on a clear night and see how many stars you can count together as a family.

name

We've been learning about stars this week. What is your favorite thing about stars? You know what today is — it's time to share what we've learned about stars with someone else. Let's add a new page to our Science Notebook!

There are many stars in the sky. Some stars burn hot. These stars are blue or white. Color this star blue!

Some stars don't burn as hot. These stars look red. Color this star red!

Some stars aren't the hottest, and they aren't the coldest either. These stars look yellow or orange. Color this star yellow or orange!

Let's read Psalm 147:4-5

He determines the number of the stars and calls them each by name. Great is our Lord and mighty in power; his understanding has no limit. What do you think that verse means?

Draw a picture of the moon and stars.

Constellations

4th Day of Creation

Learn

This week, we're continuing our adventure through the fourth day of creation as we learn more about stars. Are you ready to go? Let's talk about groups of stars we call constellations.

On a clear night, there are many, many beautiful stars to see in the sky. People have looked at and studied the stars since God created the world. People learned to see and recognize certain stars, where they are in the sky, and the way they move across the sky as the earth rotates around and orbits the sun.

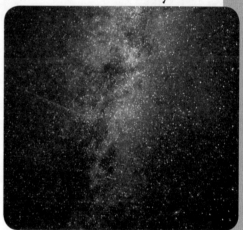

Have you ever laid on your back in the grass and watched the clouds float by as you used your imagination to think of what that cloud might look like? Maybe you've seen a cloud that was shaped like a flower or a cloud shaped like an elephant. You can use your imagination to think of something the cloud shape looks like.

When we look at the stars, we can use our imagination to connect the stars into shapes — like a dot-to-dot puzzle. People have used their imaginations to connect the stars into shapes that we can recognize and find in the sky. We call them "constellations." Can you say that word with me? Constellations.

Remember in our last story, Cain and Abel were counting the stars with Adam and Eve? Let's continue our story as we learn about constellations. Start your imagination!

Bible-inspired stories

Cain and Abel giggled. They had counted so many stars! Through giggles, Abel said, "Okay, Cain, now tell me about the pictures you can see in the stars with your imagination!"

Cain looked up at the sky. He was searching for a group of special stars. "See those three stars right there?" Cain pointed up to a line of three stars that appeared close together. "It looks like one of our belts! There are other stars above and below. If I connect them with my imagination, I see a man."

"Ooh," Abel replied, "I like this game!"

"Look over there. See that really bright star? If we connect those seven stars, it looks like a scoop in the sky." Cain pointed up to the bright star.

"Cain, look!" Abel exclaimed. "There is a big scoop too that looks almost the same! See those other seven stars?"

"I have not connected those stars yet. They do look the same!" said Cain.

"Let's see if we can imagine any other shapes in the sky!" Abel said as they each looked at the sky and imagined shapes and animals in the stars.

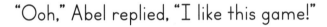

Constellations are pictures we imagine in the sky as we connect the stars. Constellations can help us find special stars. In our story, Cain pointed out the three stars in a line that look like a belt. These stars are part of a constellation that we call Orion. If you can find these three stars in the sky, you can find the Orion constellation!

Cardstock or index card	✓
Pushpin or pencil	
Flashlight	

Weekly materials list

There are two special stars in the Orion constellation. One is named Betelgeuse (pronounced "beetle juice"). You can find this star in Orion's shoulder here:

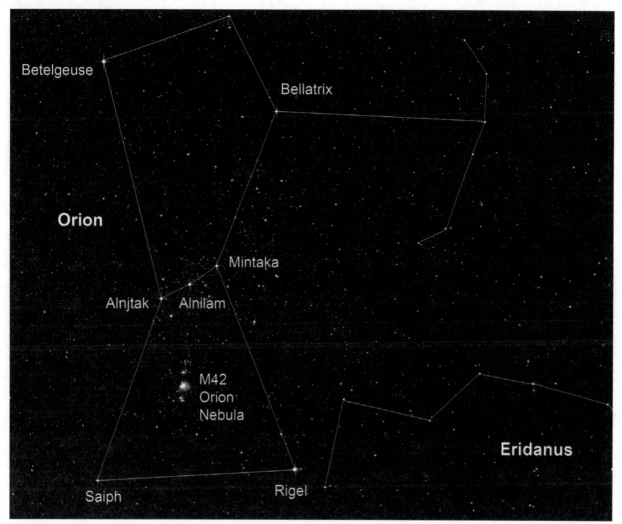

Betelgeuse is a special star because it is one of the biggest stars that we know about. It is much, much bigger than our sun, and it is very far away from us. Another special star in Orion's constellation is called Rigel, and it is one of Orion's feet.

Rigel is a very bright star in the night sky. This star's light looks like a mixture of blue and white, which tells us this star burns very hot, even hotter than our sun. The next time there is a clear dark night, see if you can find the Orion constellation in the sky. Remember to look for the three stars in a line next to each other. Once you find the Orion constellation, see if you can find Betelgeuse and Rigel!

Two other special constellations are called the Big Dipper and the Little Dipper. These constellations look like scoops, or ladles, in the sky. One is big, and the other is smaller. The Little Dipper has a special star called the North Star.

Explorers, sailors, and travelers have used the North Star to help them find the right direction to travel in. Once a person sees the North Star in the sky, they can tell if they are traveling north, south, east, or west, and that helps them travel the right way to get where they want to go.

There are many other constellations and groups of stars in the sky. One group of stars is called the Pleiades. The Pleiades star group and Orion are even mentioned in the Bible in Amos 5:8 (NIrV). Let's read that verse!

The LORD made the Pleiades and Orion. He turns midnight into sunrise. He makes the day fade into night.

He sends for the waters in the clouds. Then he pours them out on the surface of the land. His name is the LORD.

name

There are many neat things to learn about stars. Stars are amazing, and God created them on the fourth day of creation. Can you use your imagination to connect the stars on this page? What picture do you see in the stars?

Discussion Starters ▸

Have you ever looked at the night sky?

What do the stars remind you about God?

Can you think of any other special stars mentioned in the Bible?

Read Matthew 2:1–12.

Experience

materials needed

☐ Cardstock or index card

☐ Pushpin or pencil

☐ Flashlight

Today, we are going to make our own constellations on the wall! Let's get started.

Activity directions:

1. Choose a constellation from the examples below (or you are welcome to find others!) and use the pushpin to create holes in the index card in the same pattern as the constellation. The holes do not need to be exact, just a representation of the constellation.

2. Take the index card and flashlight into a dark room and shine the flashlight onto the index card to see the "stars" appear on the wall.

3. Create another constellation on a new index card and repeat.

ORION

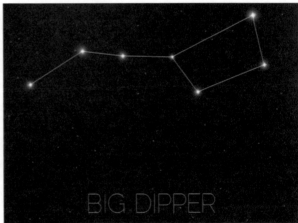

BIG DIPPER

LITTLE DIPPER

That was a lot of fun! There are many stars in the night sky, and there is so much more we can learn about them. The beauty and the number of stars in the sky remind us how powerful God is. He created the stars that we see in the night sky — and He created you, too. God knows each of the stars, even though we can't count them all, and He knows you, too. That's an important thing to know and remember. Every time you see the stars at night, you can thank God for reminding us that He loves us, He sees us, and that He cares for us.

Discussion Starters ►

Go outside at night and look at the stars for a while. There are apps you can download on your phone as well that will help you find the constellations.

Can you identify any constellations?

Trace the constellations below.

Share

name

Wow! We've learned so much about the sun, moon, and stars as we've studied the fourth day of creation. I've had so much fun, and now it's time to add a new page to our Science Notebook!

When we study the sun, moon, and stars, thcy rcmind us about God's glory and how amazing He is. The sun, moon, and stars are bigger and farther away than we can even imagine — and God created each and every one of them. Psalm 19:1 (NIrV) says,

The heavens tell about the glory of God. The skies show that his hands created them.

That is a good verse to remember when we look at the stars! Trace the verse to remind you that the sky shows us how amazing God is. Next, color the worksheet and add it to your Science Notebook. Don't forget to tell someone about the constellations you've learned about.

Trace Psalm 19:1 (NIrV)

The heavens tell about the glory of God. The skies show that his hands created them.

The Fifth Day of Creation

5th Day of Creation

Day

Learn

We've had so much fun exploring the sun, moon, and stars as we learned about the fourth day of creation the last few weeks. What was your favorite thing that you learned?

So far, we've learned about the first, second, third, and fourth days of creation. On the first day, God made the heavens, earth, and light. On the second day, God made the sky. Then, on the third day of creation, God made the land and plants. On the fourth day of creation, God made the sun, moon, and stars. Wow — we've explored so much of God's creation already!

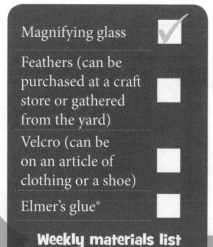

Are you ready to continue our creation adventure? Let's explore the fifth day of creation! I have a question: What did God make on the fifth day of creation? Do you wonder, too? Where do you think we should look for the answer to our question? The Bible! Let's continue reading from Genesis.

God said, "Let the seas be filled with living things. Let birds fly above the earth across the huge space of the sky." So God created the great sea creatures. He created every kind of living thing that fills the seas and moves about in them. He created every kind of bird that flies. And God saw that it was good. God blessed

Magnifying glass	✔
Feathers (can be purchased at a craft store or gathered from the yard)	☐
Velcro (can be on an article of clothing or a shoe)	☐
Elmer's glue®	☐

Weekly materials list

them. He said, "Have little ones so that there will be many of you. Fill the water in the seas. Let there be more and more birds on the earth." There was evening, and there was morning. It was day five (Genesis 1:20-23; NIrV).

I heard our answer. Did you hear it, too? On the fifth day of creation, God made living things to fill the seas and birds to fly in the sky. Are you excited to explore the creatures that live in the sea and the birds that fly in the sky? Me too!

Hmm, I wonder if Abel ever asked his mom and dad about the fifth day of creation. What do you think? Let's imagine he did!

Imagine That!
Bible-inspired stories

It was a brand new day. Abel was walking down to the stream to fill his jar with water to take back to his Mom, Eve. He glanced up at the sky as he walked and saw three sparrows flying along together. They looked like they were playing together as they flew, then they gracefully landed in a bush not far from Abel.

After they landed, they began to chirp happily. Abel giggled to himself. He liked the birds. He decided he would ask his Mom and Dad about birds after gathering water, but first, he wanted to know what God had made on the fifth day of creation.

Abel dipped his jar into the cool stream and let the water fill it up. Then, he carried the water back to their tent as he listened to the faint sound of the sparrows still chirping happily.

Adam came by as Abel was pouring the water into the big jug in their tent. "Dad, what did God make on the fifth day of creation?" Abel asked.

"Ah, on the fifth day of creation God created all the creatures that fill the sea as well as every kind of bird," Adam replied.

Abel was excited! He wanted to learn more about the creatures in the sea and about birds. "Can you tell me more about the sea creatures and the birds, Dad? I saw some birds flying just a bit ago, and I'd like to learn more about birds!"

"Yes, I can tell you about birds. It looks like the big jar will need some more water to fill it. Let's walk down to the stream together to gather more water, and we'll talk about birds as we walk." Adam rubbed his hand across Abel's hair playfully.

"Ok, Dad," Abel giggled, "let's go!"

I'm excited to learn more about birds and sea creatures with you, too! Let's talk about birds. Do you have a favorite kind of bird?

There are many kinds of birds — some are big, and some are small. Can you think of a big and small type of bird? An ostrich is a big bird, and a hummingbird is a very small bird. Some birds can fly, but other types of birds stay on the ground. Can you think of a bird that doesn't fly? A penguin is one type of bird that doesn't fly.

name

Birds are covered in feathers, and they are very interesting to learn about. This week we will explore bird feathers, but first let's connect the dots to finish the picture on our worksheet. Then, trace the words "God made birds"

Connect the dot-to-dot, then color the picture.

K J •I •H L M N• O P •G Q• F •E •D B •C R• S T A

Trace the words.

God made birds.

Discussion Starters

What is your favorite sea creature?

What did God make on the fifth day of creation?

Do all birds fly?

228

Experience

materials needed

- ☐ Magnifying glass
- ☐ Feathers (can be purchased at a craft store or gathered from the yard)
- ☐ Velcro (can be on an article of clothing or a shoe)

Teacher tip: Be sure to save the feathers from today's activity. The student will need them to complete their Science Notebook page at the end of this week.

Can you think of something special birds have? Feathers! Let's talk about feathers today and explore the design God gave them. Pick up a feather. What do you see? Can you describe it for me? Is it long or short? Is it soft? What color is the feather? [Spend time observing and describing the feather.]

Let's learn about the parts of a feather. Do you see the long hard part that runs down the middle of the feather? That is called the shaft. It is strong enough to help the feather stay straight, but very light so that the bird is not too heavy to fly. [Pinch one side of the feather at the top and move your fingers down to separate barbs] Do you see the individual strands in the feather? Each strand is called a barb.

At the very bottom of the shaft, where the feather ends, is called the quill. You may also see fuzzy, downy feathers near the quill. Now, stand your feather up on the quill and put your fingers at the top of the feather. Pinch your fingers together with the feather in between them, then slide your fingers down the feather from top to bottom — see if you can separate the barbs into strands.

What happened? Did the barbs separate easily, or did they separate into chunks? It's not easy to separate each individual tiny barb, is it? Now, pinch your fingers together at the quill and slide

barb

shaft

quill

your fingers back up. Do the barbs all go back together? If the feather still looks a bit messy, you can use your fingers to slide over just that messy section. Can you make the feather look neat again?

Why do you think the feathers are hard to pull apart individually but easy to slide back together? [Allow student to answer.] God made feathers with a really special design. Along each individual barb are little hooks that connect to each other. We call them barbules. The barbules of the feather work like velcro! [Hand your student the velcro.]

Pull apart the velcro, and then put it back together again. Do you feel how it is hard to pull apart, but easy to press back together? Velcro is made just like a bird's feather — it locks together. Pull apart the feather barbs again and look at the feather under a magnifying glass. See if you can find the barbules! They are very small and may look fuzzy in the magnifying glass. They can be hard to see!

The barbules make sure the feather can stay strong and straight to help the bird fly. Birds make sure the barbs on their feathers are stuck together by using their beak. This is called preening. See if you can use your fingers to pinch all the feather barbs back together like a bird would.

When birds preen their feathers, they also apply oil on their feathers. Oil and water don't mix together, so the oil helps the bird's feathers stay dry. Feathers are pretty amazing, aren't they?

 **Discussion Starters** ▶

Identify parts of a feather.

How are velcro and a bird's feather similar?

Hold a feather under a stream of water for a few seconds and then pull it out. Ask your student: Is the feather soaked or did the water roll off it? Oil helps to protect the feather. If the feather absorbed water or became too wet, the bird wouldn't be able to fly. God gave birds a special design!

Day

Share

name

We're learning about the fifth day of creation this week! Do you remember what God created on the fifth day? God created the creatures in the sea and the birds on the fifth day of creation.

materials needed

☐ Elmer's glue®

☐ Craft feathers (or feathers gathered from the yard)

Glue feathers to the worksheet

Teacher tip: If the feathers are too long, you may trim them to fit the worksheet.

Blank for gluing.

Birds

5th Day of Creation

Day

Learn

It sure was interesting to study bird feathers, wasn't it? I'm ready to learn some more about birds, how about you? Let's talk about flight!

God created many kinds of birds to fly. Have you ever watched a bird fly high up in the sky? Can you think of any special ways God may have designed birds so that they can fly? One way God designed birds specially is their bones. You and I have bones inside of us. They are hard, and they help us do things like stand, walk, or throw a ball. Our bones are heavy. God gave the bird very light bones, though. They are specially designed so that the bird can fly.

God also gave birds very strong muscles so that they can flap their wings and keep them spread apart to fly. The feathers on a bird's wings are important, too. Remember how we saw the barbs link together and stay smooth? When a bird flies, the air glides smoothly over and under the wing. If the feathers were ruffled and messy, it would be hard for the air to move smoothly over the wings. God gave feathers their special design to keep them smooth so that air can pass over them and the bird can fly.

A bird's tail is also very important. Do you have any ideas why? Hmm, how do you think the bird can steer itself when it is flying? Its tail! The bird moves its tail to steer itself in the direction it wants to fly. How neat!

Of course, God also made some birds that are not able to fly, but He gave them other special abilities! The ostrich is a type of bird that cannot fly. The ostrich can be between 8–10 feet tall. That is taller than an adult! An ostrich has powerful legs that can run over 40 miles an hour. Have you ever seen an ostrich at a zoo?

Can you think of another type of bird that cannot fly? I'm thinking of one that is black and white and usually lives where it is cold. Do you know what it is? A penguin! Penguins are also not able to fly, but God gave them a different special ability. Do you know what it is? They are graceful, fast swimmers! On average, penguins swim at about 7 miles per hour, which is about as fast as a bottlenose dolphin usually swims.

Option A:

Toilet paper or paper towel cardboard roll, or a pinecone ✓

Peanut butter ☐

Birdseed ☐

Yarn or twine ☐

Plate ☐

Butter Knife ☐

Option B:

Needle and thread ☐

Unbuttered, unsalted popcorn ☐

Apples and oranges cut into pieces ☐

Berries, if desired ☐

God made many types of birds, and each type is unique. Some have bright and beautiful colorings, others are plainer. Each has a special design and purpose. Sparrows are small, plain birds, but Jesus talked about them in Matthew 10:29–30:

Are not two sparrows sold for a penny? Yet not one of them will fall to the ground outside your Father's care. And even the very hairs of your head are all numbered.

That verse tells us that God cares for the sparrows even though they are small and people may not place much value in them. It reminds us that God cares for us, too. He even knows how many hairs are on your head! When you see a bird or hear one chirp, let it remind you that God cares for it and that He cares much more for you.

Discussion Starters ▶

Do you think a bird has to have strong muscles to be able to fly?

How long can you flap your arms or hold them out to your sides before your muscles become tired?

- Go for a drive at 40 miles per hour to see how fast an ostrich can run.

- Look up a video online of an ostrich running or a penguin swimming. Be sure to preview the content first and then enjoy with your student.

Experience

I like to watch birds, how about you? Today, let's make a bird feeder and hang it up outside. Then, we can watch the birds that come to enjoy the food! We can watch them eat and fly away. How many different kinds of birds do you think we'll see? Let's make our feeder, and then we can find out. I'm excited to watch the birds eat and then fly!

materials needed

Option A —
Birdseed Feeder:

☐ Toilet paper or paper towel cardboard roll, or a pinecone

☐ Peanut butter

☐ Birdseed

☐ Yarn or twine

☐ Plate

☐ Butter knife

materials needed

Option B—
Garland Feeder

☐ Needle and thread

☐ Unbuttered, unsalted popcorn

☐ Apples and oranges cut into pieces

☐ Berries, if desired

Activity directions:

Option A-Birdseed Feeder

1. Attach a piece of yarn or twine to the toilet paper roll or pinecone. It should be long enough that you can hang the completed feeder on a branch.

2. Spread peanut butter on the toilet paper roll or pinecone.

3. Spread a layer of birdseed on the plate, then roll the toilet paper roll or pinecone through the seed so that the layer of peanut butter is covered in seed.

4. Go outside and hang up your feeder. Keep an eye on it through the next few days and see if you see any birds (or other wild critters) enjoying a snack!

Option B-Garland Feeder

1. Carefully thread the needle and cut a foot or two of thread for the length of the garland.

2. Help your student carefully slide the first piece of fruit over the needle, then slide the fruit to the end of the string and tie a knot around it to secure. Be sure to leave enough string on the end to tie the garland to a branch.

3. Continue helping your student slide popcorn, fruit, and berries over the needle until the garland is full. Tie a knot around the last piece and be sure to leave enough string on the end to tie the garland to a branch.

4. Go outside and hang up your feeder. Keep an eye on it through the next few days and see if you see any birds (or other wild critters) enjoying a snack!

Discussion Starters ►

Watch the bird feeder. How many types of birds do you see come to it?

What types of birds do you have around in your area?

What type of bird is your favorite?

- Have your child draw a picture of the birds that come to the feeder.

- Purchase a bird-watching book. When your child sees a bird, help him or her look it up in the book to identify it.

Share

I'm having so much fun learning about birds! It was fun to learn how birds fly this week and make a bird feeder so that we could watch the birds around us. Did you see any take off and fly?

Do you know what today is? It's time to add a new page to our Science Notebook and share what we've learned with someone else! States and countries have special flags, and sometimes they also choose a type of bird and a flower. Find out your state or national bird and draw a picture of it on the next page. Then, copy the words "God made birds special."

The northern cardinal is the state bird of seven states.

The western meadowlark is the state bird of six states.

Tear out for Science Notebook

name

Draw your state bird.

Trace and copy the words "God made birds special."

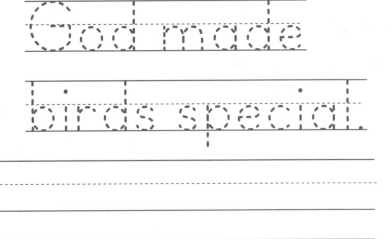

Draw a picture of your favorite bird.

Bird Nests

5th Day of Creation

Day

Learn

Have you ever been walking outside and noticed a bird's nest in a tree or shrub? What was it made of? What shape was it? Were there any baby birds inside? [Allow student to answer.] Have you ever gotten to hold a bird's nest in the fall after the bird is done using it? Do you think you could build a nest like that?

Birds' nests are often quite amazing little things. They have a big job to do and have to remain strong to protect the eggs and baby birds in all kinds of weather. God designed the bird to know just how to build the perfect nest! I think that is pretty neat!

I'd like to explore bird nests this week, so let's get started! In our last story, Adam and Abel were walking to the stream to gather some more water to fill the big jar in the tent. Let's imagine what happened next as Abel discovers a bird's nest!

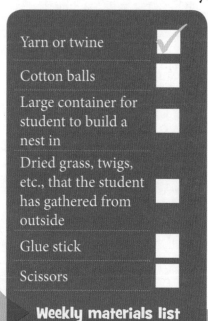

Yarn or twine	✓
Cotton balls	☐
Large container for student to build a nest in	☐
Dried grass, twigs, etc., that the student has gathered from outside	☐
Glue stick	☐
Scissors	☐

Weekly materials list

Imagine That!

Bible-inspired stories

Adam and Abel walked to the stream together to fill their jars. On their way, Abel heard the little sparrows still chirping quite happily. He ran up to the tree they were sitting in now, and he noticed a bird's nest! One of the sparrows was sitting on her nest.

Adam noticed the nest, too. "What did you find?" he quietly asked Abel so that they didn't scare the bird away.

"It's a bird's nest! Look at it," Abel said quietly, but still very excitedly. "It's beautiful! All that grass and the twigs are right in place so that they can hold together. How does the bird know what to do?"

"Ah, that is instinct. God created the birds, and He put inside them the things they would need to know how to do. A bird knows just how to create a nest. It gathers grasses, twigs and sticks, and other materials to build its nest. It may also use mud to stick everything together. Then, little by little, the bird builds its nest!"

Just then the little sparrow flew away. "Let's see if she has any eggs in the nest," Adam said as he lifted Abel up onto his shoulders. Abel peeked inside the nest. It was so carefully made! He squealed in delight when he saw them — two little birds sitting safely within the nest. Adam set him back down. "Let's leave the nest now so the bird comes back."

"Okay!" Abel said. And with that, they slowly walked away from the tree toward the stream to fill their jars.

A bird gathers dried grasses, twigs, mud, spider webs, feathers, and other materials it can find to build its nest. Little by little, the bird will gather and fly the materials to the spot it has chosen to build its nest. As it builds, it will shape the nest so that it is just right for holding and protecting its eggs. Some birds build tiny nests, others — like the bald eagle — build very large, very heavy nests.

Once the nest is complete, the bird will lay its eggs in the nest. The bird will then sit on the eggs in the nest to keep them warm. This is called incubation. The eggs have to be kept warm so that the baby bird inside can begin to grow. Some baby birds will grow quickly and be ready to hatch in about two weeks, while other birds will continue growing inside the egg for over a month!

When the time is just right, the baby bird will begin to peck the shell from the inside to crack the egg. God gave baby birds a special tool on their beak to help them peck and crack the egg open. It is called an "egg tooth." How amazing! It is hard work for the baby bird to open the shell! Finally, the bird will open the shell all the way, and it hatches. Then, the mother or father bird will fly out to find food for the babies. Once they find food, they'll fly back to the nest to feed their babies.

The baby birds will continue to grow and develop in the nest until they are too big to stay in the nest. We call these baby birds fledglings. The fledglings may leave the nest and spend a few days on the ground as the mother and father bird teach them important things. Then, the fledgling will begin to fly! The bird has grown from an egg to an adult bird.

Someday, maybe that baby bird that grew up will build a nest of her own for more baby birds. This is called the bird life cycle. Have you ever seen baby birds inside their nest? Have you heard them chirping for food in the nest? God designed the birds to know just how to care for their babies.

Discussion Starters

- Find a time-lapse video online of a bird building a nest and enjoy with your student.
- Find a video of a baby bird hatching and enjoy watching with your student.
- ◀ Search online for images of bird nests. Look up a bald eagle nest, sparrow's nest, a weaver nest, and a goose nest.

What looks different?

What is similar?

A bird knows just how to construct a nest. Some birds create very large nests, while other nests are quite small. I have an idea! Let's try to make our own bird's nest today! Ready to give it a try?

Experience

materials needed

☐ Yarn or twine

☐ Cotton balls

☐ Large container for student to build a nest in

☐ Dried grass, twigs, etc., that the student has gathered from outside

Activity directions:

1. Go outside with your student and gather dry grasses, twigs, sticks, mud (optional), feathers, and any soft materials you can find.

2. Begin to construct a nest in the container.

3. You can use the yarn to help hold it together and pull apart the cotton balls to create a soft layer if desired.

Wow, that was neat! Tell me about your nest.

Is it big or small?

Was it harder or easier to make than you expected?

Do you think a bird works hard to create its nest?

Why or why not?

Discussion Starters

• Look up recipes for edible bird nests and make one with your student.

• Explore nature around you.

Can you find any old bird nests in a tree or on the ground?

This bird is watching her nest. Can you draw and color the eggs in the nest?

Share

It's been so much fun learning about birds with you this week! We learned about bird nests, eggs, and baby birds. Do you know what it's time to do today? Add a new page to our Science Notebook!

Don't forget to tell someone about a bird's life cycle and their amazing nests!

Cut out the pictures of the bird life cycle, then glue them to the worksheet in the right order.

materials needed

☐ Glue stick

☐ Scissors

Blank for cutting life cycle of a bird.

name

The life cycle of a bird.

1

2

3

4

5

6

Answer key for the life
cycle of a bird.

Layers of the Ocean

5th Day of Creation

Day 1 Learn

Shh, do you hear the sound of ocean waves crashing against the sand? Let's imagine we do! What does the ocean sound like? Can you make a sound like the ocean waves? The ocean is an incredible part of God's creation, and we're going to explore it this week!

God made the earth on the first day of creation, and it was covered in water. On the third day of creation, God gathered the water together into one place and called it a "sea." The flood in Noah's time changed the earth, though, so things look a little different today.

Today, there are many seas and five oceans on the earth. The seas aren't quite as deep as the ocean and are located near land. The ocean is deep and vast. The names of the oceans are Indian Ocean, Arctic Ocean, Pacific Ocean, Southern Ocean, and Atlantic Ocean.

Just like the atmosphere and the inside of the earth, we also organize the ocean into layers that help us study and explore it. Each layer in the ocean is home to very unique creatures. We'll learn about those later on as we continue to explore the fifth day of creation! For now, let's explore the layers of the ocean together!

Materials	✓
Mason jar or big glass container	✓
Glass container for mixing	
Funnels	
Syringe	
Corn syrup	
Water	
Vegetable oil	
Blue food coloring	
Dark blue dish soap	
Rubbing alcohol	
½ or ¼ measuring cup	

Weekly materials list

Let's get into a pretend submarine and explore the ocean!

Sunlit zone (ocean's surface to 656 ft)

Twilight zone (656 ft to 3,280 ft)

As we start our adventure, our submarine will first explore the top layer of the ocean. We call the first layer of the ocean the sunlit zone. Can you guess why we call this first layer the sunlit zone? [Allow student to answer.]

We call this layer the sunlit zone because the light from the sun shines through this layer. This layer is home to many sea creatures that we'll be learning about later on! The sunlit zone can be as deep as 656 feet. That is very deep in the ocean, but the ocean can be far deeper than that!

As we travel deeper through the ocean, eventually the sunlight will begin to fade, and it will get darker and darker. The sunlight is very filtered and faint in this zone of the ocean. We may even feel totally in the dark. We call this the twilight zone.

There are really neat things to learn about and study in the twilight zone. Some of the fish that live in the twilight zone actually have a special ability to make their own light! God's creation is amazing, and we'll meet those creatures later on in our ocean adventures! The twilight zone goes down to about 3,280 feet.

Are you ready to continue exploring deeper into the ocean? Next, we reach the midnight zone! The midnight zone stretches from 3,280 feet to 13,123 feet deep. This zone is also extremely dark — no sunlight reaches this zone. The water from above is very, very heavy and it presses down hard on the creatures that live in this zone. God designed creatures that can live in the very cold temperatures and under the high pressure of this zone of the ocean.

Let's keep diving even deeper! Now we've reached the abyss at 13,123 feet deep. This zone is very cold, around 32 degrees Fahrenheit, and the pressure from the water is even stronger here. This makes it very difficult for scientists to study this zone of the ocean. But, even here, God created special creatures that can live and thrive in these extreme conditions.

Finally, the deepest part of the ocean is called the trenches. These are deep holes in the ocean floor formed by earthquakes and volcanoes during the Genesis Flood. This area of the ocean is also very hard for scientists to study and learn about because it is so deep and the pressure of all that water above it is very strong.

It's time to come back up to the surface now. Do you remember what this is called? The sunlit zone! That was a fun adventure through the ocean zones. We're going to learn a little more about each zone as we continue our adventures through the fifth day of creation!

Midnight zone
(3,280 ft to 13,123 ft)

Abyss zone
(13,123 ft to 19,685 ft)

Trenches

name

Discussion Starters ► Search online for a video of a styrofoam cup traveling deep into the ocean. As the cup crushes and sinks, explain it is the high water pressure that crushes the cup as it goes deeper and deeper. But, God created special creatures that can withstand those high pressures!

Trace the ocean zones.

sunlit zone

twilight zone

midnight zone

abyss zone

trenches

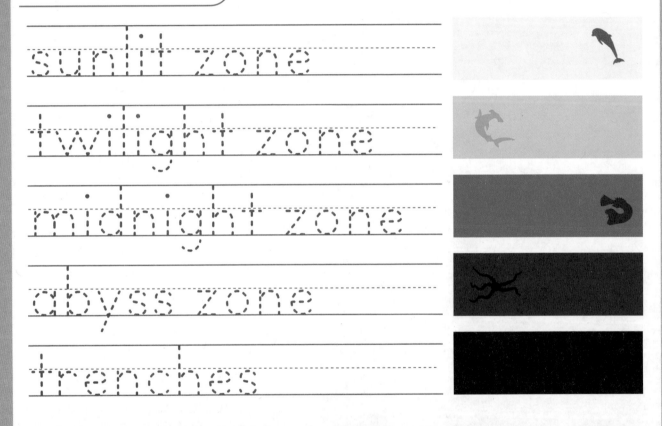

Experience

materials needed

☐ Mason jar or big glass container

☐ Glass container for mixing

☐ Funnels

☐ Syringe (one from a child's liquid medicine will work well)

☐ Corn syrup

☐ Water

☐ Vegetable oil

☐ Blue food coloring

☐ Dark blue dish soap

☐ Rubbing alcohol

☐ ½ or ¼ measuring cup, depending on the size of your jar

We've been learning about the layers in the deep blue ocean! Today, we're going to make our own ocean layers in a jar. This will be so much fun!

Activity directions:

1. Measure ½ or ¼ cup of corn syrup and pour into your mixing container. Add several drops of blue food coloring to make the syrup a deep, dark blue — this will be our trench layer.

2. Pour the corn syrup into the mason jar, using a funnel if needed.

3. Measure ½ or ¼ cup of dish soap. Pour the soap carefully into the mason jar so that it rests on top of the corn syrup, using a funnel if needed. This layer represents the abyss.

4. Next is the midnight zone! Measure ½ or ¼ cup of water and pour into your mixing container. Add a couple drops of food coloring so that the water is deep blue, but not as dark as the dish soap layer.

5. Use the funnel and pour the water into the mason jar very slowly and gently so that it doesn't mix with the soap (or so that mixing is very minimal).

6. Next up is the twilight zone! Measure ½ to ¼ cup of vegetable oil and pour the oil into the mason jar very slowly and gently.

7. Finally, use the syringe to slowly dispense rubbing alcohol as the final layer.

8. Observe the layers you've created!

Discussion Starters ▶

Can you name the layers of the ocean?

Can you tell me about a layer of the ocean?

Which layer are you most excited to learn about?

Have you ever been to a beach and stood at the edge of the ocean? There is so much water and God made many unique creatures to live there.

Let's color the picture of the beach.

Share

name

What a fun adventure we've had this week through the layers of the ocean! I'm excited to learn more about the creatures God placed in the ocean as we continue our studies. Today, though, it's time to dry ourselves off from all that ocean water and add a new page to our Science Notebook. Don't forget to tell someone else about the layers in the ocean, too!

Cut out the ocean zones on page 259 and glue them below in the right order.

Blank for gluing.

Twilight zone

Trenches

Abyss zone

Sunlit zone

Midnight zone

Blank for cutting out ocean zones.

The Sunlit and Twilight Ocean Zones

5th Day of Creation

Learn

Let's go on another science adventure! God made the birds and the sea creatures on day five of creation. There are many types of sea creatures and fish that live all over the world! Some fish live in a river, stream, pond, or lake — these are usually called freshwater fish. Freshwater is water that isn't salty like the ocean. A few types of freshwater fish are catfish, crappie, goldfish, and even some kinds of eels live in freshwater. Have you ever gone fishing and caught a freshwater fish?

Other types of fish live in saltwater like the ocean or sea. A few types of saltwater fish would be clownfish, jellyfish, sharks, and manta rays. If you have a fish tank at your house, you most likely have freshwater fish living there, but you can also have a saltwater fish tank that can hold fish from the ocean. Today, we're going to explore the sunlit and twilight zones of the ocean and learn about some of the amazing saltwater fish God created to live there. Are you ready to go swimming? Grab your pretend scuba diving gear, and let's jump right into the ocean!

We'll start our adventure in the sunlit zone. Light from the sun filters down through the water in this zone. The sunlit zone of the ocean is home to many amazing and beautiful fish and sea creatures. Can you think of a sea creature you might see jump out of the water at an aquarium show? I'm thinking of a bottlenose dolphin! A bottlenose dolphin is a sea creature that must come to the surface to breathe air.

Another sea creature that lives in the sunlit zone and comes to the surface to breathe is the orca, or killer whale. Killer whales are designed for swimming very fast — up to 30 miles per hour! God made the killer whale and dolphin with a special way to breathe. You breathe through your nose, but a dolphin and a killer whale have a hole at the top of their heads to breathe through. This is called a blowhole. Because the blowhole is at the top if its head, the dolphin or killer whale doesn't have to put its whole face out of the water to breathe — just the top of its head. That means the killer whale or dolphin can keep swimming while it breathes because it can poke just the top of its head out of the water.

There are many more types of creatures that breathe air, but we have more of the ocean to explore! The sunlit zone of the ocean is also home to many types of fish. Fish do not have a nose or a blowhole. How do you think they get the oxygen they need? God designed fish with gills. These are like little slits on the sides of the fish. When the fish opens its mouth, water travels through its mouth and out the slits of its gills. The gills are specially designed to be able to

Sink or bathtub full of water	✓
Fork	
Spoon	
Construction paper	
Scissors	
Elmer's glue® or glue stick	
Crayons or markers	
Glitter (optional)	

absorb the oxygen from the water, and also to push carbon dioxide back out into the water — kind of like when you exhale carbon dioxide. Isn't God's design amazing?

Some fish help each other. Fish and turtles need help to clean themselves — even big, tough fish like sharks sometimes need help! God made a special group of fish we call cleaner fish to help the bigger fish stay clean. A cleaner fish removes and eats any dead skin or parasites on the fish.

Sharks will come and open their mouths wide for the cleaner fish to come inside and start to clean. The cleaner fish will help to clean inside the shark's mouth, and the shark will not eat the cleaner fish. The cleaner fish gets to eat a good meal while it cleans, and the shark gets all cleaned up! The shark and the cleaner fish help each other. This is called a symbiotic relationship — it means they can both help each other.

The twilight zone is deeper in the ocean, and very little sunlight reaches this layer. You can find many types of sea creatures living in this ocean layer like crabs, some types of jellyfish, eels, and even some kinds of octopus! One unique fish that lives in the twilight zone is called the lanternfish. Can you think of why it may have that name? God made the lanternfish with a special ability to make light, like a lightning bug! We're going to learn more about fish that make light next week. It's going to be so much fun!

Of course, there are many, many other types of fish and creatures in the ocean! We can only explore a few today. But wasn't it fun learning a little more about some of the sea creatures that live in the sunlit and twilight zones of the ocean?

name

God made the sea creatures on the fifth day of creation. Can you draw a picture of your favorite sea creature?

Discussion Starters

What colors do you see?

Is the fish saltwater or freshwater?

Can you spot the fins and their gills?

What fish is your favorite?

⬆ Take a field trip to an aquarium or a pet store with fish tanks. Observe the fish you see.

• Pick a saltwater or freshwater fish to learn more about. The *Aquarium Guide* available through Answers in Genesis or Master Books is a great resource to start with!

• Search for a video of a cleaner fish helping another fish or shark and watch it with your student.

How do you think you could help someone else?

Experience

materials needed

☐ Sink or bathtub full of water

☐ Fork

☐ Spoon

Fish swim in water, and God designed them perfectly for swimming! Fish have fins and tails to help them turn in the water and swim fast. Let's do an experiment to learn how fins help fish swim through the water!

We're going to use a fork first and move it through the water. Then we'll use a spoon. Do you think the fork or the spoon will move water around better? You think the _____ will move
[fill in with student's answer]
water around better. Do you remember what this is called? Your hypothesis!

Activity directions:

1. Instruct student to hold the fork with the prongs facing down and lower the prongs into the water.

2. Instruct student to move the fork back and forth slowly through the water. Can they feel the water push back against the fork? Does the fork move very much water around or does it seem to "cut" through the water?

3. Now try the spoon. Instruct the student to hold the spoon and lower it into the water. Then, slowly move the spoon back and forth through the water. Can they feel the water push back against the spoon?

4. Repeat, but have the student use their hands. First, instruct them to spread their fingers wide like a fork. What do they feel as they move their hand through the water?

5. Now have them close their fingers together and help them to slightly scoop their hands — as if they were going to go swimming. Then, instruct them to move their scooped hand through the water. What do they feel?

That was fun! Did the fork or the spoon move water around better? [Allow student to answer.] Is that what you thought would happen? The fork and your open fingers let the water slide right through them. This design wouldn't help you swim very far or very fast, would it?

The spoon and your scooped hand are solid surfaces, which means the water can't slide right through — it pushes back against it. Did you feel the water push back against the spoon as you moved it? Have you ever gone swimming and used your hands and feet to help you move through the water?

A fish's fins are like the spoon and your cupped hands. They help the fish push against and move through the water. A fish's fins and tail can have many shapes and sizes, but they all help the fish swim and turn in the water exactly how God created them to. What an amazing design God gave fish!

● ● ● ● ● ● ● ● ►
Discussion
Starters

Have you ever gone swimming?

How do you use your hands and feet like a fish's fins to help you move through the water?

Have you ever been in a canoe or kayak?

What did you or your parent use to help you move through the water?

Can you tell me how that is also like a fish's fins?

267

Share

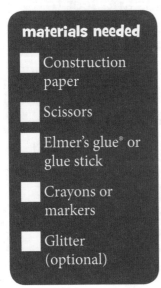

materials needed

- [ ] Construction paper
- [ ] Scissors
- [ ] Elmer's glue® or glue stick
- [ ] Crayons or markers
- [ ] Glitter (optional)

This week was so much fun learning about the sunlit and twilight zones of the ocean and a few of the creatures we find there! Which creature was your favorite to learn about? Well, today it is time to add a new page to our Science Notebook and share what we've learned with someone else!

God made fish on the fifth day of creation. He designed fish with fins and tails to help them swim and gills so they can breathe underwater. Let's cut fins and a tail out of our construction paper, decorate them, and then glue the fins and tail to our fish on page 269. Then, be sure to draw the gills as well! What will you name your fish?

Teacher tip: Help your student design, cut out, and decorate fins and a tail for their fish.

name
_____

Name of my fish:

_____
[fill in with student's answer]

Blank for gluing.

Deep-sea Creatures

5th Day of Creation

Day Learn

It's time for another science adventure this week! We've been learning about the zones of the ocean, do you remember the names of any of the zones? [Allow student time to answer.] We call the ocean zones sunlit, twilight, midnight, abyss and trenches.

Can you think of some things fish have that we've already learned about? [Allow student time to answer.] We've learned about fins, tails, and gills. We've also learned about the sunlit and twilight zones of the ocean. Let's explore the deepest parts of the ocean this week - are you ready? What do you think we will find if we dive even deeper?

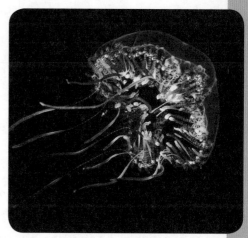

Do you think the creatures will be big or small deeper in the ocean? Do you think they will be very colorful or rather plain? Do you think they will look similar or different from each other?

I can't wait to find out! Hmm, do you think Adam ever wondered about the sea creatures God made? Let's imagine he did!

Clear 1-liter soda bottle	✓
Glow stick bracelet or glow in the dark paint	☐
Construction paper	☐
Permanent marker	☐
Scissors	☐
Tape	☐

Weekly materials list

Imagine That!
Bible-inspired stories

Abel sat by the stream. He was by himself, thinking about God's creation. As he thought about all the things he had been learning, a small fish jumped up from the stream then plopped back under the water. Abel looked down into the stream to see the fish swim below the water. He liked to watch the fish swim.

Adam saw Abel sitting there and walked over from their tent to sit with Abel. "What are you doing, buddy?" Adam asked as he sat down.

"I'm just watching the fish swim and thinking about all the things I've learned about God's creation. I sure do like watching the fish!" Abel replied happily.

"I like to watch the fish, too. Out beyond this stream is the sea. There are many more types of fish and sea creatures there! There are many different types of creatures God made to live on land. Can you imagine how many amazing creatures there must be deep in the sea? I asked God about them one day —"

Just then, Abel interrupted, "Can you tell me about what you learned?"

Adam laughed. "Yes, I was just getting to that part! There are many sea creatures, big and small. Some must come to the surface to breathe air just like us, and others God designed to be able to get the oxygen they need from the water. There are creatures God designed to live close to the surface, and others He designed to live deep down at the very bottom of the sea."

"Can we plan a trip to the sea, Dad? Maybe we'll be able to see some of the creatures God created to live in the water!" Abel exclaimed.

Adam thought for a minute. "Yes, I think we can do that! Let's go talk to Mom and decide when we can walk to the sea."

As soon as Adam said that, Abel jumped to his feet and ran toward the tent. He could not wait to go to the sea and look for creatures God had created to live there!

God designed creatures to live in the very deepest parts of the ocean. Let's learn a little bit about a few of these creatures. We call these creatures deep sea fish. We'll start in the midnight zone! This layer of the ocean stretches from about 3,300 feet to 13,200 feet below the ocean's surface. There is darkness all around in this zone and a lot of pressure from all the water above and around. God made creatures designed to live in, or dive deep down to, the midnight zone.

One sea creature that can dive down all the way to the midnight zone is the sperm whale. The sperm whale needs to breathe air from the surface through its blowhole. However, the sperm whale can hold its breath for an hour and a half so that it can dive all the way down to this dark zone of the ocean. Can you imagine being able to hold your breath that long? A sperm whale is bigger than a school bus, and it needs to eat a lot of food. The sperm whale likes to eat giant squid that live in the twilight and midnight zones of the ocean.

Because there is no sunlight this deep in the ocean, most creatures in the midnight, abyss, and trenches zones of the ocean are blind and don't have bright colors. The sunlight does not reach these deep zones of the ocean, but you may still see lights. How can that be? Well, some types of fish in these zones make their own light, kind of like a lightning bug. We call this bioluminescence. What a big word! Can you say it with me? Bioluminescence.

The anglerfish is an interesting fish that can make light. It has a glowing lure at the top of its head that it uses to attract other fish that it can eat. A similar fish is the viperfish that also has a glowing lure that it flashes to attract prey. The viperfish also has very long teeth!

There are so many interesting fish deep in the ocean. Let's keep exploring! Deep in the ocean, you may find jellyfish, squid, crabs, and perhaps a dumbo octopus. The dumbo octopus has large fins on the side of its head that look kind of like elephant ears. It uses its fins to swim through the water. The dumbo octopus has tentacles like the octopi you usually see in pictures, but this octopus' tentacles are webbed, so it looks a bit more like an umbrella when the octopus opens them.

We're not done exploring yet! Remember when we learned about the layers of the earth and how it gets very hot deep in the center of the earth? Sometimes, there are cracks on the floor of the ocean that let water travel deeper into the earth where it gets very hot. The super-hot water is then let back into the ocean through hydrothermal vents.

The water around the hydrothermal vent is dark and very cold — almost freezing! But the water that comes out of the hydrothermal vent is extremely hot — hotter than boiling water. There are creatures like tube worms and the hydrothermal vent octopus that like to live even there! God designed many types of sea creatures. Some can live near the surface, and others can live deep down where it is cold and dark. Didn't God make amazing creatures?

name

There are many creatures deep in the ocean!
Help the sperm whale dive deep down.

Discussion Starters ►

How long can a sperm whale hold its breath?

Set a timer for an hour and a half to find out!

What is a hydrothermal vent?

Experience

We've been exploring the deepest parts of the ocean, and we've learned about some of the unique creatures God made to live there! Some types of deep-sea fish create light. They are bioluminescent. Let's create our own bioluminescent glow-in-the-dark fish today!

materials needed

- [ ] Clear 1-liter soda bottle
- [ ] Glow stick bracelet or glow in the dark paint
- [ ] Construction paper
- [ ] Permanent marker
- [ ] Scissors
- [ ] Tape

Activity directions:

1. If using glow in the dark paint, first paint the soda bottle and allow to dry.

2. Follow the packaging directions to start the glow sticks (if using) and slip one or two inside the soda bottle, then tightly screw on the lid.

3. Use the permanent marker to draw eyes on this fish.

4. Cut out fins from the construction paper and tape them on the fish.

5. Take the fish into a dark room and watch it glow.

Discussion Starters

What would you name your glowing fish?

What do you think of the fish God created to live deep in the ocean?

name
_____

We've had quite an adventure through the ocean as we've explored the deepest parts and a few of the creatures God created to live there. It's time to add a new page to our Science Notebook. Are you excited? There are many different types of creatures God created to live in the ocean. Some can live at the very top, and others live deep down. Let's trace and color these ocean creatures and add this page to your Science Notebook. Don't forget to tell someone about the amazing fish God created to live in the ocean!

Draw a picture of your favorite fish. Be sure to show someone and tell them about how God made this fish unique!

The Sixth Day of Creation

6th Day of Creation

Day

Learn

What an adventure we've been on through the days of creation! We've learned about the first day of creation when God made the heavens, earth, and light. What is your favorite thing about light? Then, we learned about the second day of creation, when God made the sky — the atmosphere! Next, we learned about the third day of creation when God made dry ground and plants. Do you remember something you learned about plants?

After that, we learned about the fourth day of creation when God made the sun, moon, and stars! Then came day five when God filled the ocean with creatures and also made the birds. It was fun to learn about sea creatures and birds!

Now it's time to learn about the sixth day of creation! Are you excited? I know I am! I wonder . . . what did God make on the sixth day of creation? Do you wonder, too? Where should we take our question? The Bible! Let's read about the sixth day of creation in Genesis 1:24–31. God created a lot on this day, so listen carefully!

And God said, "Let the land produce living creatures according to their kinds: the livestock, the creatures that move along the ground, and the wild animals, each according to its kind."

Scissors	☑
Glue stick	☐

Weekly materials list

And it was so. God made the wild animals according to their kinds, the livestock according to their kinds, and all the creatures that move along the ground according to their kinds. And God saw that it was good.

Then God said, "Let us make mankind in our image, in our likeness, so that they may rule over the fish in the sea and the birds in the sky, over the livestock and all the wild animals, and over all the creatures that move along the ground."

*So God created mankind in his own image,
in the image of God he created them;
male and female he created them.*

God blessed them and said to them, "Be fruitful and increase in number; fill the earth and subdue it. Rule over the fish in the sea and the birds in the sky and over every living creature that moves on the ground."

Then God said, "I give you every seed-bearing plant on the face of the whole earth and every tree that has fruit with seed in it. They will be yours for food. And to all the beasts of the earth and all the birds in the sky and all the creatures that move along the ground — everything that has the breath of life in it — I give every green plant for food." And it was so.

God saw all that he had made, and it was very good. And there was evening, and there was morning — the sixth day.

Wow! I heard our answer. Did you hear it, too? What did God make on the sixth day of creation? God made the animals and a man and woman — this was Adam and Eve!

There are so many amazing things to learn about on the sixth day of creation. Let's start with the animals. In Genesis 2:19–20, we learn that Adam gave each animal and bird a name. Let's read about it!

Now the LORD God had formed out of the ground all the wild animals and all the birds in the sky. He brought them to the man to see what he would name them; and whatever the man called each living creature, that was its name. So the man gave names to all the livestock, the birds in the sky and all the wild animals.

Can you imagine naming the animals? God made many kinds of creatures. Some are really big, and some are really small. What is your favorite kind of creature God made on day six and what would you have named it?

Animals have a family group or kind just like the Bible says. Let's talk about the dog animal kind. Dogs can be big or small, one color or several colors. Some dogs have stripes while others have spots. They may have long hair or short hair. Some we can keep as pets, and others — like wolves — stay wild.

Even though each dog is a little different, we still can see and know it is a dog — and it will always be a dog. A dog would not change into an elephant or a cat, because God made it to be a dog. God gave each kind of creature variety, but they each stay in their kind. Dogs are dogs, cats are cats, and elephants are elephants!

Cats are another animal kind. There are small cats that we keep as pets and big wild cats like a lion or tiger. Each can look different, but they are all part of a cat kind. Another animal family kind are bears. Can you think of some different types of bears? There are brown bears, polar bears, black bears, giant pandas, and more! Each is different, but each is part of the bear family kind.

God designed the animal kinds on day six of creation, and we can see His creativity in all the different types of animals we see in each family kind. Let's use our creativity! There are many types of dogs on your worksheet. Can you color each one a little differently?

name _____

Color the dog kinds.

Discussion Starters

Choose an animal family kind to explore deeper with your student.

Can you think of any more animal family kinds?

Do you have a pet?

What makes your pet unique or a special animal?

Is your pet a wild animal or friendly animal?

Day

Experience

We're learning about day six of creation and animal kinds this week! God made the animals on the sixth day of creation, and He gave them variety within their animal kind. Let's cut out the animal pictures from our manipulative page and then sort them into their kinds!

Activity directions:

Teacher tip: Save the animal cards from this lesson for the student's notebook.

materials needed

☐ Scissors

1. Help your student cut out the animal cards from page 287.

2. Sort out the animal cards into their family groups — dog, cat, bear, rodent, and lizard.

3. Observe similarities and differences within that kind.

Discussion Starters

Go on a field trip to the zoo.

Can you find any animal kinds such as different types of bears or wild dogs?

Share

materials needed

☐ Animal cards from prior lesson

☐ Glue stick

name

_____

We're learning about the sixth day of creation, and it's time to add a new page to our Science Notebook today! This week, we learned that God created the animals and a man and woman on the sixth day. We've been learning that God created many kinds of animals. A kind is the family group an animal belongs to, like the dog kind or the cat kind.

God gave each kind variety, so they can each look a little different from each other, but they always stay in their kind. What was your favorite animal kind from our activity day? Let's sort our animal cards from page 287 into each animal kind and glue them to our worksheet. Then, add this page to your Science Notebook!

God made the dog kind on day six of creation.

God made the cat kind on day six of creation.

God made the bear kind on day six of creation.

God made the rodent kind on day six of creation.

God made the lizard kind on day six of creation.

Blank for cutting out animal cards.

Animal Habitats

6th Day of Creation

Day

Learn

Moo, baa, roar, woof, meow! God made many different kinds of animals on the sixth day of creation. Let's read Genesis 2:19-20 again and imagine what it must have been like!

Now the LORD God had formed out of the ground all the wild animals and all the birds in the sky. He brought them to the man to see what he would name them; and whatever the man called each living creature, that was its name. So the man gave names to all the livestock, the birds in the sky and all the wild animals.

Wow! It must have been really cool to be Adam and give each animal and bird a name. What do you think Adam may have named the elephant? Or a duck? Or a cat? What would you have named them?

Do you think Cain and Abel ever asked Adam about what it was like to name all the animals and birds? Let's imagine that they did and that Adam told them all about the sixth day of creation!

Container to hold habitat	✓
Animal toys belonging to one habitat your student chooses: arctic, rain forest, forest, or desert	☐
Materials to build a habitat for the toys (e.g., ice for arctic, sand for desert, etc.)	☐

Weekly materials list

Imagine
That!
Bible-inspired stories

"Boys!" Adam called out. "Come help me tend the flocks."

"Coming, Dad!" Abel and Cain replied as they walked toward Adam and the small flock of sheep.

This would be a good time to ask Dad what God made on the sixth day of creation, Abel thought to himself. "Hey, Dad? What did God make on the sixth day of creation?" he asked.

"It must have been the animals, and Mom and Dad!" said Cain excitedly.

"That's right!" Adam replied. "On the sixth day of creation, God made the animals and your mom and me. There are many kinds of animals, and each kind is pretty amazing. You know I got to name the animals, right?"

"Really, Dad?" Abel asked.

"Yes, God brought the animals and birds to me and asked what I'd like to name them. There were so many kinds of animals — each unique. I was amazed by God's design! But it turned out, God wasn't done creating yet. I was tired after naming all the animals, and I fell asleep. I fell asleep harder than I've ever slept!"

Abel and Cain giggled, "Did you snore, Dad?"

Adam laughed. "I don't know, but God did something amazing while I slept. He took one of my ribs and from that He created your Mom. When I woke up, your mom was there, and I was so happy! I said,

"This is now bone of my bones
and flesh of my flesh;
she shall be called 'woman,'
for she was taken out of man"
(Genesis 2:23).

"It sure was an amazing day! Let's go gather water for the sheep, and I'll tell you some more about the animals I named." Adam grabbed the boys' hands as they walked together to grab the jars to carry water. He was excited to tell his sons all about his favorite animals.

What is your favorite animal? What do you think you would have named it? Let's learn a little more about the animals today. Do you remember when we learned about the continents? After the flood of Noah's time, the earth and weather were different. The animal kinds spread out all over the earth. God gave each animal kind variety, and some animal kinds are created very well to live in certain places. We call these places habitats. A habitat is the place an animal can live, like the ocean, desert, forest, rain forest, or the arctic.

Some animals can live very well in the cold environment of the arctic. Can you think of what the arctic habitat is covered with? Ice and snow! It is very, very cold there, and the animals that live there must be able to survive in the extreme cold. Can you think of any animals that may live in the arctic?

Polar bears, penguins, and walruses are a few animals that can live there! Many animals that live in the arctic have a thick layer of fat. This helps to keep the animal warm in the very cold temperatures.

The desert is another type of habitat. The desert is very hot during the day but very cold at night. There is also very little water in the desert because it does not rain often. Animals in this environment need to be adaptable to temperatures that change, and they also need to be able to live with very little water.

One animal that can live very well in the desert is the camel. Camels have feet that can easily walk through sand and long eyelashes to protect their eyes from blowing sand. They can close their nose so sand doesn't blow in, and they can store water in the fat of the hump on their back. Camels have a great design for living in the desert!

Another habitat is the forest. Can you think of any animals that live in the forest? You may see a lot of squirrels, chipmunks, or deer in a forest. Bears are another animal you may find in the forest! Animals in the forest need to be able to survive the seasons: spring, summer, fall, and winter. Animals such  as squirrels gather food during the summer, so they'll have something to eat in the cold winter when food is harder to find. Forest animals also need to be able to stay warm in the cold winter months, so many kinds grow a warm, thick coat of fur before winter comes. In the spring when it warms up, the extra fur will fall off so that the animal isn't too hot in the summer — what a neat design!

 The rain forest, or jungle, is also a habitat. The rain forest is warm, and there is plenty of water. There are many plants and trees in the rain forest. There are so many types of animals and brightly colored birds that live here. Can you think of any? What about chimpanzees, tigers, macaws, and sloths? Chimpanzees can swing through the trees, and there are a lot of trees in the rain forest! There are many rain forests around the world, and many types of animals live there. They are specially designed to live in a warm, wet habitat.

Each habitat is different, and there are animals that have a special design to help them live there. It is really neat to explore the world and learn about the animals God created, isn't it?

Teacher tip: Ask your student which is their favorite habitat: rain forest, desert, forest, or arctic? Gather some animal toys that would live in this habitat and set aside for the activity this week. Also think of materials you could use to build a habitat for those animals (e.g., ice cubes for the arctic, grass or pine needles for the forest, leaves to build a rainforest, sand for desert, etc.; ideas may also be found online).

desert   jungle   arctic   forest

●●●●●●●●●►
Discussion Starters

Cover your child's finger with a thick layer of butter, then have them dip the covered finger and an uncovered finger in cold water. The butter acts like fat, helping to keep the covered finger warm.

Which finger gets cold first?

What kinds of animals can be found in that habitat?

What ways are they specially designed to live there?

← Pick a habitat to study deeper.

Day

It's really neat to learn about animal kinds and their habitats! God created many kinds of animals, and some are designed to live very well in different habitats. Let's build a habitat for a group of animals today!

Experience

materials needed

- [ ] Container to hold habitat

- [ ] Animal toys belonging to one habitat your student chooses: arctic, rain forest, forest, or desert

- [ ] Materials to build a habitat for the toys (e.g., ice for arctic, sand for desert, etc.)

Activity directions:

1. Help your student choose animal toys that belong to one habitat: arctic, rain forest, forest, or desert.

2. Ask your student what they might find in that habitat? (e.g. ice, grass, trees, etc.) What can they use to build a habitat for the toys?

3. Gather materials and help your student build a habitat in the container.

4. Ask your student to put the animals in the habitat they've created! What animals live in that habitat? Can your student think of any ways the animals are specially designed to live there?

Discussion Starters

What is your favorite animal?

What habitat does it live in?

Can you think of any other habitats (e.g., ocean, pond, etc.)?

Where do you live?

What is the temperature like?

Share

name

It has been so much fun learning about animal habitats this week! Are you ready to add a new page to our Science Notebook? Let's get started! We learned about the desert, arctic, jungle, and forest habitats. Can you draw the habitat for each group of animals?

desert habitat

arctic habitat

jungle habitat

forest habitat

Mankind

6th Day of Creation

Day Learn

Learning about animal habitats sure was fun! Do you remember what else God made on the sixth day of creation? God made mankind — human beings — on the sixth day of creation! Let's read Genesis 1:26–27 again:

Then God said, "Let us make mankind in our image, in our likeness, so that they may rule over the fish in the sea and the birds in the sky, over the livestock and all the wild animals, and over all the creatures that move along the ground."

So God created mankind in his own image, in the image of God he created them; male and female he created them.

God made people different and unique from the animals because people are made in the image of God. What do you think that means to be made in the image of God? [Allow student to answer.] To be made in God's image means that He made us to reflect His traits. We call those traits the attributes of God. Attribute is a big word that means the qualities, traits, or character of someone or something. For example, you are _____ . This is one of your attributes.

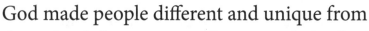

[fill in with one of your student's character traits]

2 straws	✓
Tape or rubber bands	☐
2 paper bags or gallon-sized Ziploc® bags	☐

Weekly materials list

Can you think of a few of God's attributes? The Bible tells us that God is love, He is merciful, and that He is just. We can also see in creation that God is creative, detailed, and organized. God has many other attributes as well. When we are loving, creative, or merciful, we reflect the image of God!

But, remember how sin broke the world? Because of sin, people are broken just like the world, and they don't always reflect God's traits very well because of sin. Sometimes, people are not loving or merciful. When they are not loving or merciful, they are not reflecting the attributes of God. Instead, they are reflecting the attributes of sin, and sin is a very sad thing. Sin hurts us, and it hurts other people.

It's really neat that God made us in His image! Let's talk about some of the other special ways God made people. God designed our bodies with many parts and systems that all work together. Let's read Genesis 2:7 to find out how God made man:

Then the LORD God formed a man from the dust of the ground and breathed into his nostrils the breath of life, and the man became a living being.

Do you know who that man was? It was Adam! But what about Eve? Let's read a little more from Genesis 2:21–23:

So the LORD God caused the man to fall into a deep sleep; and while he was sleeping, he took one of the man's ribs and then closed up the place with flesh. Then the LORD God made a woman from the rib he had taken out of the man, and he brought her to the man.

The man said,
"This is now bone of my bones
and flesh of my flesh;
she shall be called 'woman,'
for she was taken out of man."

Do you know the name of the woman God made? Her name was Eve! Let's learn more about the special systems God made for our bodies. Take a deep breath in, now breathe out — I think we should talk about breathing first!

Remember when we talked about photosynthesis and how plants make oxygen? Your body needs oxygen. Oxygen is part of the air around us. When you breathe in, you inhale air, which contains the oxygen your body needs. When you breathe out, you exhale carbon dioxide that your body doesn't need.

Breathe in all the way again — now breathe out. That cycle of breathing in and breathing out is called a breath. A six-year-old takes about 18–30 breaths a minute, without even thinking about it. That means if you breathe 18 times in a minute, you'll take 25,920 breaths in a day while you are playing, resting, sleeping, eating — all the things that you do during the day. How amazing!

If you are running, your body needs more oxygen, so you will breathe faster — and you don't even have to think about it! Take another breath in. Can you feel where the air enters your body? It enters through your nose, or it can also come through your mouth. The air passes through your nose or mouth, then travels through your trachea. The trachea can also be called the windpipe, and it's like a straw that carries air where it needs to go.

So, where does that air need to go in your body? To your lungs! You have two lungs. They expand when you breathe in as they fill with air, and they get smaller as you breathe out. The trachea carries air to your lungs where it passes into the bronchi. The bronchi look a little bit like the branches of a tree, and they also carry the air to where it needs to go — just like the trachea.

At the end of the bronchi are very small air sacs called alveoli that pass the oxygen to your blood so it can be used. The alveoli also take the carbon dioxide so that you can breathe it out. What an amazing design that God gave our bodies!

This is called the respiratory system, and it is just one of the many systems in your body. You breathe air in through your nose or mouth. The air travels through your trachea to your lungs, where the air sacs or alveoli inside can pass the oxygen to your blood so that it can be used by your body. Then, the air sacs also receive the carbon dioxide that your body doesn't need so that you can breathe it out when you exhale. Let's trace the names on the respiratory system!

name

Trace the words below. Ask your parent to read each word as you trace it.

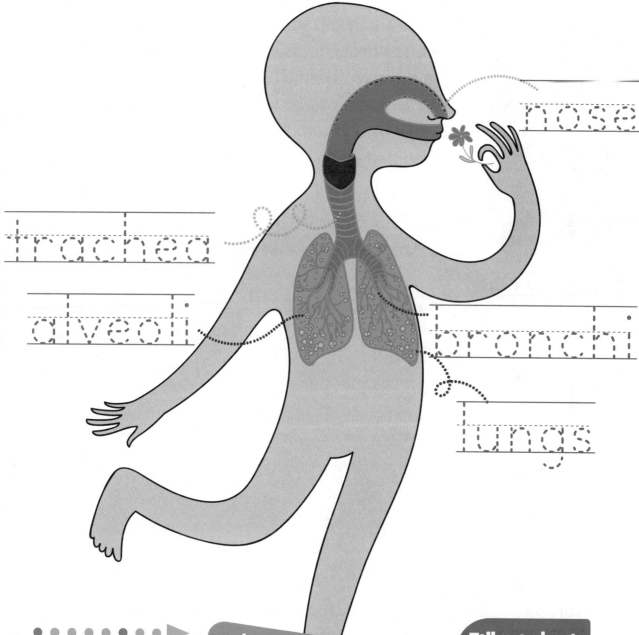

nose

trachea

alveoli

bronchi

lungs

•••••••••►
Discussion Starters

Then, jump or run around for a little while.

Count how many breaths you take in a minute.

How many breaths do you take in a minute after that?

Tell me about what happens when you breathe in.

Where does the air go?

Experience

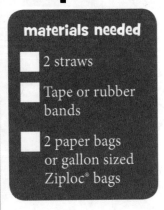

materials needed

☐ 2 straws

☐ Tape or rubber bands

☐ 2 paper bags or gallon sized Ziploc® bags

Learning about the respiratory system sure has been fun! Do you remember how the respiratory system works? First, you breathe air in through your nose, then the air travels through your trachea to your lungs. The bronchi inside your lungs then carry the air to the alveoli, which pass the oxygen to your blood so that it can be used by your body. The alveoli also take the carbon dioxide that your body doesn't need so that you can breathe it out.

You have two lungs. They expand when you breathe in and get smaller when you breathe out. Let's make a model of what that looks like!

Activity directions:

1. Open the paper or Ziploc® bags and place one straw at the opening of both, leaving a couple inches of the straw exposed outside the bag.

2. Use the tape or rubber bands to secure the bag to the straw.

3. Direct your student to put both straws in their mouth. Then, have them take a deep breath in and blow out through the straws.

4. As they blow out, the bags will expand as they inflate with air. Explain that this is what their lungs look like inside when the student breathes in.

5. Now, breathe in once through the straws to deflate the bags. Explain that this is what their lungs look like inside when the student breathes out.

That sure was neat to see the bags expand as they filled with air and then get smaller as the air left! Psalm 150:6 tells us, *"Let everything that has breath praise the LORD. Praise the LORD."* What a good reminder! You and I have breath. Can you think of something we can praise the Lord for today?

Discussion Starters

How much air can your lungs hold?

- Take a deep breath in, then blow up a balloon as you exhale. Compare the balloon with a parent's or sibling's balloon.

- Show a parent or sibling your lungs from our activity and tell them about how God designed your respiratory system.

Let's memorize

Psalm 150:6

"Let **everything** that has **breath** praise the **LORD**. **Praise the LORD**."

	Actions
everything	Hold your hands palms up and sweep them through the air as if gesturing to everything or everyone in the room.
breath	Point to your nose.
LORD	Make an L with your pointer finger and thumb on your left hand. Place your left hand at your right shoulder and cross it in front of you to your left hip — almost like you are wearing a sash and tracing over it with your hand. You can also search for this sign online to see it in action by searching "sign language for Lord."
Praise the LORD	Place your hands together in prayer or raise them in worship

Day ···

Share

name

Today is an exciting day! It's time to add a new page to our Science Notebook. Remember what the lungs look like? Let's draw the lungs to complete the respiratory system.

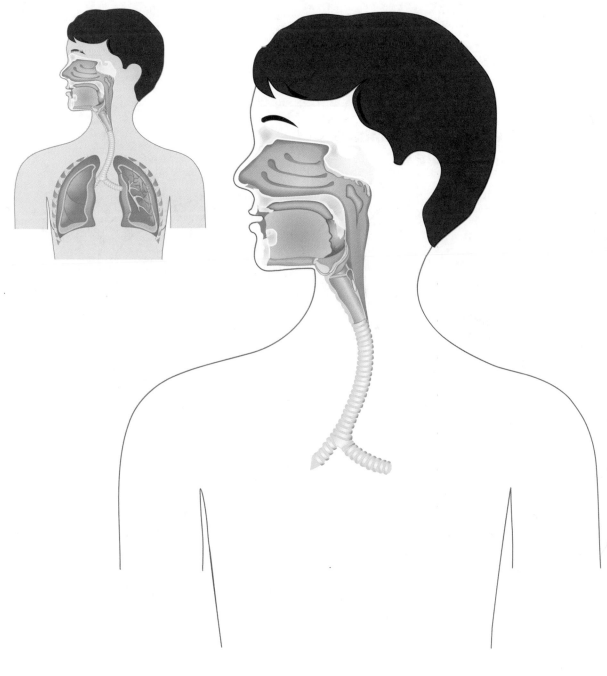

Trace Psalm 150:6.

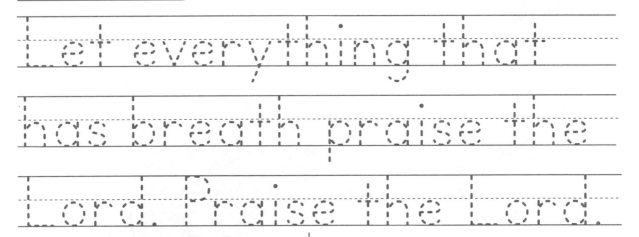

Let everything that has breath praise the Lord. Praise the Lord.

Color these important reminders of things you should do.

read your Bible

pray

sing praise

tell others about Jesus

The Circulatory System

6th Day of Creation

Learn

Welcome back for another science adventure! We're learning more about the human body this week as we study some of the amazing systems in your body. Last week, we learned about the respiratory system. Can you tell me about what happens to the air after you breathe it in?

You breathe air in through your nose, and it travels through your trachea to your lungs. Inside your lungs, the bronchi carry the air to the alveoli, which pass the oxygen to your blood. Then, your blood carries the oxygen to where it needs to go in your body. The alveoli also receive the carbon dioxide that your body doesn't need so that you can breathe it out when you exhale.

Do you wonder how the blood can travel to where it needs to go in your body? Let's talk about it! Your blood carries nutrients from the food you eat and oxygen from the air you breathe to all the parts of your body. Your blood travels through veins and arteries. Veins and arteries are like little tubes — like a garden hose — that carry the blood where it needs to go in your body. Arteries carry blood that has received oxygen from your lungs, and your veins carry blood that needs to get new oxygen. Turn your wrist over. Can you see the veins and arteries traveling under your skin?

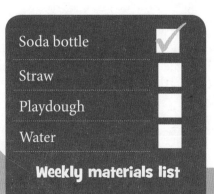

Soda bottle	✓
Straw	
Playdough	
Water	

Weekly materials list

The blood in your body needs something to help it travel through your veins. Blood can't travel on its own. Can you think of what helps the blood travel through your veins and arteries? Here's a hint: beat, beat, beat. It's your heart! God made the heart to pump blood through your body, and it is a pretty amazing creation.

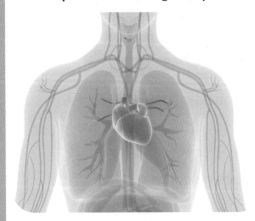

Your heart is tucked inside your chest and is about the same size as your fist. Make a fist with your hand. That's about how big your heart is! The heart is very strong, and it pumps blood through your body all day and all night, every day! The heart needs to help the arteries move the blood that has oxygen, and it needs to help the veins move the blood that needs to get oxygen. Let's explore how it does those jobs!

First, the blood in your veins needs to get rid of carbon dioxide, and it needs to receive oxygen from the alveoli in your lungs. The blood starts at the heart and comes in at the top on the right side. This is called the right atrium. The heart then pumps the blood down to the bottom right — it's called the right ventricle. The heart keeps pumping and pushes the blood out to the lungs where it can receive oxygen.

Now the blood is in your lungs where it can pass the carbon dioxide for you to exhale and receive oxygen — but it still needs to get that oxygen to the rest of your body! So, the heart keeps pumping the blood to move it along. Next, the blood comes back to the heart, but this time, it comes in through the left side called the left atrium. Just like before, the blood flows to the bottom of the heart, the left ventricle, and the heart pushes the blood out to the arteries and pumps it through your body. Your blood cycles through this process over and over again, isn't that neat?

This is called the circulatory system. What an amazing part of God's creation! Do you think Cain and Abel ever learned a little bit about the blood in their bodies? Let's imagine they did!

Imagine That!
Bible-inspired stories

Cain and Abel were playing a game of tag while Adam and Eve were making dinner. "Tag, you're it!" Cain giggled as he tagged Abel. But just as Cain turned to run away, he tripped over a big rock. He fell so hard, he scraped his knees on the dirt, and another sharp rock made a small cut on his arm. Ouch!

Cain started to cry as Abel helped him up. "Are you okay? Ow, it looks like your arm and knees must hurt!" Abel saw Cain's arm was bleeding a little. "Mom, Dad! Cain got hurt!" he called as both boys walked back toward the tent.

Eve wet a cloth and used it to clean up Cain's cuts and scrapes. The small cut on his arm continued to bleed for a little while.

"Hey Dad, what's that red stuff on his arm?" Abel asked.

"That is blood. Your heart pumps the blood through your body, and the blood delivers oxygen and nutrients where they need to go," said Adam. "The blood travels through your body in small tubes called veins and arteries." Adam turned his wrist over and pointed out the lines traveling under the skin. "See? These are carrying blood where it needs to go in my body."

"Whoa!" both boys said as they looked at their own wrists.

"Sometimes when you get hurt, it makes a little cut in one of the veins or arteries, and you bleed, just like Cain's arm is now. But, the blood will begin to stick together — this is called clotting. The blood will start to clot and make a seal over the little hole and the cut on the skin. This helps to stop the bleeding, and it also helps to protect it. Soon, the blood will harden into a scab, and the body will start to heal the cut."

"What a neat design God made!" Abel exclaimed.

"I just wish it didn't hurt," Cain said as he wiped the tears off his face. Cain and Abel watched the blood harden into a scab over the small cut.

"I'm very glad God is merciful and that He gave our bodies ways to heal," Eve said as she gave the boys a hug. "Go back out and play now so we can finish dinner," she said with a smile.

The circulatory system and blood sure are neat! Learning about the heart also reminds me of something in the Bible. You have a physical heart in your chest that pumps blood through your body, but sometimes we also talk about what makes you uniquely you. We call this your heart, too. In Psalm 51:10, it says, *Create in me a pure heart, O God, and renew a steadfast spirit within me.*

That verse doesn't mean your real heart needs to be cleaned up. It is talking about the part of you that makes you uniquely you. We also call this the heart of you. God sees and knows this part of you. He knows how you feel, what you think, and what you do. This part of us is broken because of sin. Psalm 51:10 reminds us to ask God to create in us a clean and pure heart, to help us stay growing strong in Him so that we can continue to reflect His image. That is a good thing to remember when you think of your physical heart!

name

Trace the parts of the human heart. Ask your parent to read the words as you trace them.

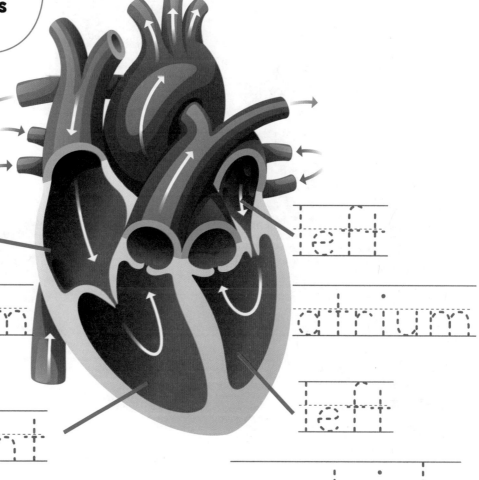

right

atrium

left

atrium

right

left

ventricle

ventricle

Discussion Starters ►

Help your student take your pulse.

Can you feel the heart pumping blood through the artery?

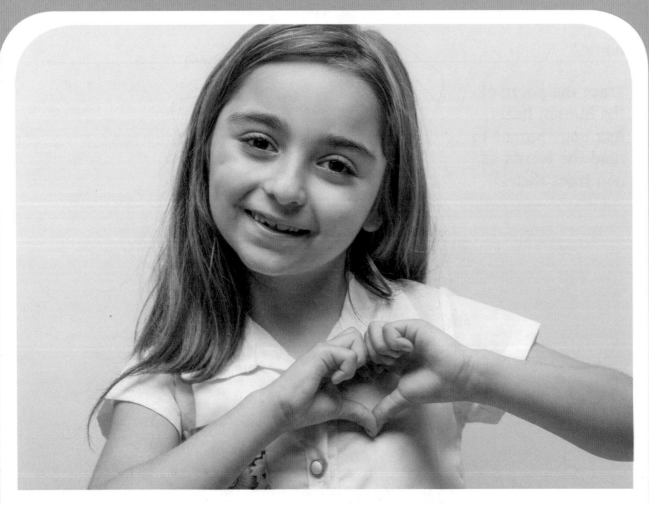

 **Let's memorize**

Psalm 51:10

"**Create** in me a pure **heart**, O God, and renew a **steadfast** spirit **within me**."

	Actions
create	Make fists and tap one on top of the other, as if you are building something.
heart	Trace a heart shape in the air.
steadfast	Stomp your feet on the ground.
within me	Place your hand over your heart.

Experience

We've been learning about the circulatory system this week. Your heart pumps blood through your body so that oxygen and nutrients can get to where they need to go. Let's make a pump to see how it can move water!

materials needed

☐ Soda bottle

☐ Straw

☐ Playdough

☐ Water

Activity directions:

1. Fill the soda bottle with water.

2. Place the straw inside the water bottle, leaving the straw to stand outside the bottle 3–4 inches.

3. Use the playdough to seal the opening of the bottle and hold the straw in place.

4. Instruct your student to squeeze the bottle (over the bathtub, sink, or a container). As they squeeze, the soda bottle will "pump" the water through the straw.

Wow, that sure was neat! When you squeeze the bottle to pump it, it moves the water through the straw. Just like when your heart pumps, it moves blood through the arteries and veins inside your body!

Discussion Starters ►

Can you explain how the heart moves blood through the body in the circulatory system?

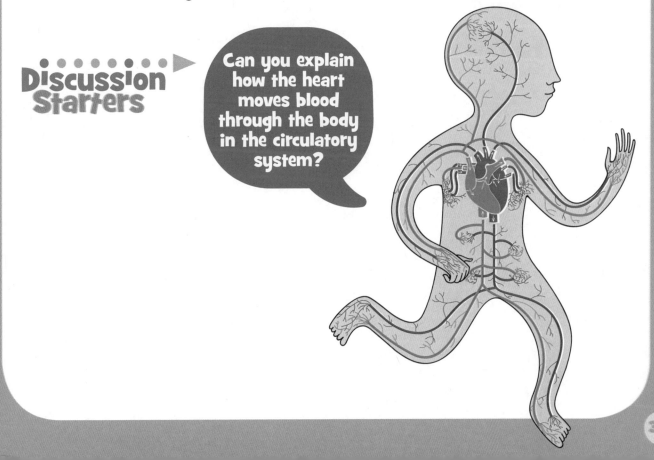

A doctor can use a stethoscope
to listen to your heart beat.
Color the stethoscope.

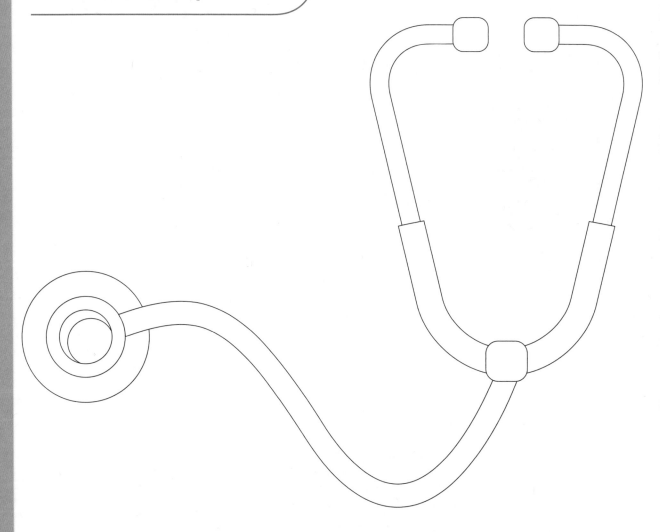

name

It's time to share what we've learned about the circulatory system this week. Let's add a new page to our Science Notebook! Your heart pumps blood through your veins and arteries. Your veins and arteries travel all through your body. Trace Psalm 51:10 then color the following page.

Trace Psalm 51:10.

Create in me a pure

heart, O God, and

renew a steadfast

spirit within me.

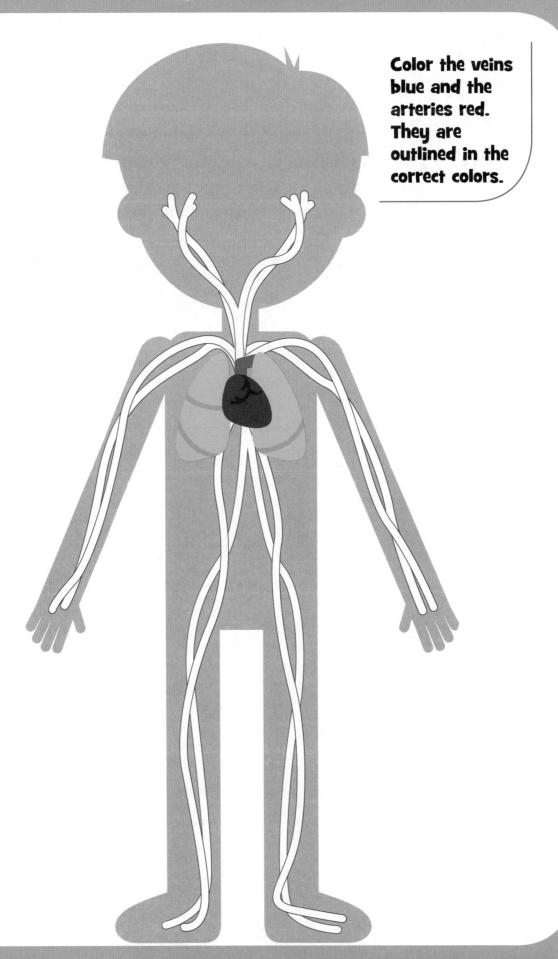

Color the veins blue and the arteries red. They are outlined in the correct colors.

Uniquely You

6th Day of Creation

Day

Learn

Wasn't learning about the respiratory and circulatory systems over the last couple of weeks really fun? God designed our bodies in some very special ways, and there are many systems in our bodies that all work together. It's so much fun to study God's creation and learn how He made us! It's time to start another science adventure this week. Are you ready to learn about a unique part of God's creation? What do you think it might be?

Well, this week we are going to learn about a special part of God's creation — you! Did you know that God made you special and unique? There is no one else quite like you, and God loves you very much! Are you ready to learn a little more about you? Let's go!

First, we want to know what God says about us. Where do you think we should start? In the Bible! The Bible says that you are fearfully and wonderfully made. Those words mean that when we study the special ways God designed us, it reminds us how amazing He is. It makes us stand in awe, amazed with God's design, and it makes our hearts want to worship Him. Let's read Psalm 139:13–14:

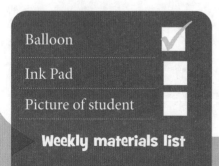

Balloon	✓
Ink Pad	
Picture of student	

Weekly materials list

For you created my inmost being; you knit me together in my mother's womb. I praise you because I am fearfully and wonderfully made; your works are wonderful, I know that full well.

These verses remind us that God created the very deepest parts of us, all the parts that make us who we are. God designed you, and He knows every part of you! Psalm 139:1–4 says,

You have searched me, LORD, and you know me. You know when I sit and when I rise; you perceive my thoughts from afar. You discern my going out and my lying down; you are familiar with all my ways. Before a word is on my tongue you, LORD, know it completely.

God knows you, and He loves you very much — He created you! God made you on purpose for a purpose, and you are a very special part of God's creation. Look at the pad of your thumb. Do you see all those lines and ridges? One way God made you unique is your thumbprint!

Your thumbprint is different from anyone else's. You and I have different thumbprints. See, look at my thumb! Our thumbs may look similar, but they are not exactly the same. Your thumbprint began to form before you were even born. That is pretty amazing. Your thumbprint is unique — it's special to just you. Isn't it amazing that there are so many people, but God makes each of us unique and loves us all?

We've learned how sin broke the world and how it hurts us and other people. Sin separates us from God, and it has a very high price. God sent Jesus to pay the price for our sin, and the price is death. Jesus died for us to pay for our sin so that we can be close to God. Then, Jesus rose from the dead. He beat sin and death! John 3:16 says,

For God so loved the world that he gave his one and only Son, that whoever believes in him shall not perish but have eternal life.

God loves the world. He loves you and me and all people. I'm so glad God loves us so much that He sent Jesus to pay the price for our sin, aren't you? Because Jesus paid the price, we can have a relationship with God when we ask Jesus to forgive our sins. We can grow in our relationship with God.

name _____

God made you special and unique. He knows you, and He loves you. That is a really neat thing to remember as we learn about your thumbprint this week! You are a special part of God's creation.

Can you draw a picture of yourself?

Read Psalm 139:1–18 together.

What are ways you can grow in your relationship with God?

Psalm 139:14

❝I **praise** you because I am **fearfully and wonderfully** made; **your** works are **wonderful**, I **know** that full well.❞

	Actions
praise	Lift your hands in a worship clap or place your hands together in prayer.
fearfully and wonderfully	Place your hands in front of you with palms facing out. Push hands back and forth in front of you.
your	Point to the sky.
wonderful	Place hands in front of you with palms facing out. Push hands back and forth in front of you.
know	Point to your forehead.

Experience

materials needed

☐ Ink Pad
☐ Balloon

You are a unique and special part of God's creation. He made you, and He loves you very much. He made each of us different, and He gave everyone a unique fingerprint. Let's look at your thumbprint a little closer today. Are you ready to get started?

Activity directions:

1. Gently tap the student's thumb onto the ink pad to apply ink.

2. Carefully stamp the student's thumb onto the balloon. (Be careful, the ink may smear easily on the balloon depending on the type of ink used. Use caution not to touch the print or smear it on a surface.)

3. Blow up the balloon. The thumbprint will get bigger as you blow.

4. Examine the thumbprint.

Wow, your thumbprint is really neat to look at! No one else has the same exact thumbprint as you. Your thumbprint is a great reminder that you are a special part of God's creation!

Discussion Starters

What are some of the ways God made you unique?

- Repeat the activity with each family member and compare them to your child's unique thumbprints.

- Purchase *The Work of Your Hand*, available from Master Books, to learn more about fingerprints as a family.

name

It's time to add a new page to our Science Notebook! What did you learn this week? [Allow student to answer.] God made you, and you are a unique part of God's creation. You are fearfully and wonderfully made. Let's add this page about you to your Science Notebook, and don't forget to tell someone else that they are fearfully and wonderfully made, too!

Trace and copy Psalm 139:14.

materials needed

☐ Ink Pad
☐ Glue stick
☐ Picture of student

I am fearfully and
wonderfully made!

child's picture here

I have _____ eyes.

I have _____ hair.

This is my thumbprint. ☐

I want to be _____ when I grow up.

One way God made me unique is:

_____

_____

The Five Senses

6th Day of Creation

Day

Learn

We've learned about some amazing systems in your body — the respiratory system and the circulatory system. Which was your favorite system to learn about? We've also learned about how God made you unique, and looked at your special thumbprint. Did you know God also gave our bodies five really neat tools to help us explore the world that He made? Can you think of what those tools might be?

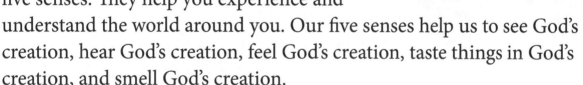

You've used some of these tools in our activities as we've talked about God's creation! The five special tools God gave us to help us learn and explore are seeing, hearing, touching, tasting, and smelling! These five tools are called your five senses. They help you experience and understand the world around you. Our five senses help us to see God's creation, hear God's creation, feel God's creation, taste things in God's creation, and smell God's creation.

Let's talk more about our five senses. Let's start with our eyes. Our eyes are specially designed to help us see the things around us. We can see lights, shapes, and colors with our eyes. Do you see the dark circle in the center of my eye? That is called the pupil. The pupil helps to make sure the right amount of light gets into our eyes. When it is really bright, the pupil is small.

| Ice cube made from fruit juice | ✓ |
| Plate | |

Weekly materials list

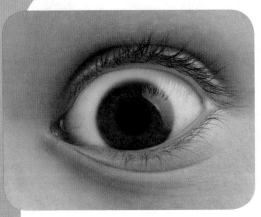

When it is darker, the pupil gets bigger to let more light in. That's a pretty neat design, isn't it?

God gave our eyes an amazing design, but because we live in a fallen world, sometimes things don't work quite the way they were designed to. Sometimes, our eyes may need a little bit of help to be able to see things clearly. God gave people wisdom to be able to create glasses that can help our eyes see things right. Other times, the eyes may not be able to see things at all because they are blind. When things don't work quite right, it reminds us that the world is broken because of sin. It also reminds us to be thankful that Jesus came to pay the price for our sin and that someday He will make everything perfect again.

Let's talk about our ears next! Our ears help us hear the people, things, or animals around us. Your ear is an amazing creation as well. The outside is shaped so that it can gather sounds from all around you and pass them to inside your ear. The sounds then move through the inside of your ear to the eardrum, and the eardrum

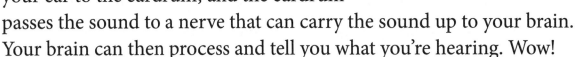

passes the sound to a nerve that can carry the sound up to your brain. Your brain can then process and tell you what you're hearing. Wow!

Just like the eyes, sometimes the ears can't hear quite right, and they need a little help. God gave people wisdom to be able to create hearing aids that can help someone hear. Other times, the ears can't hear sounds at all because they are deaf. Did you know the Bible tells us about times Jesus healed blind eyes and deaf ears when He was here on earth? We can read about it in John chapter 9 and Mark chapter 7.

Next, let's talk about touch! We can feel and touch things around us. Our sense of touch also helps to keep us safe. It tells us when something is too hot to touch. We can feel things that are soft, hard, scratchy, smooth, or sticky. What is something you feel on your skin right now?

Let's talk about the fourth special tool now, taste! We taste through our tongue. Can you see all the little bumps on my tongue? [Teacher, stick out your tongue for your student to see.] These are called taste buds. They help you taste flavors. Our tongue can taste things that are sour, sweet, bitter, and salty. What is your favorite taste?

Finally, our fifth sense is smell. We can smell the world around us. Sometimes, we can smell something really nice, like a flower or the smell of the air after it rains. Other smells aren't so nice, like a skunk! Our noses also help keep us safe. Sometimes, you can smell food that stinks, so you know it isn't good to eat anymore because it has rotted. What is your favorite smell?

The five special tools God gave us to explore and experience the world around us sure are neat!

name

Trace the words below.

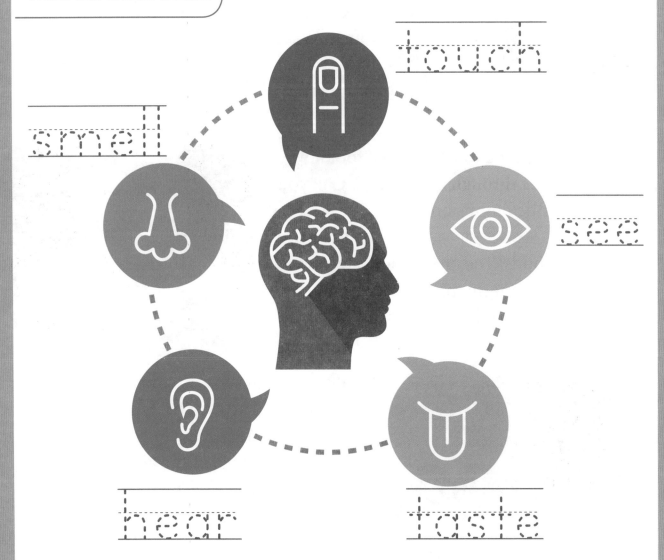

touch

smell

see

hear

taste

●●●●●●●●●►
Discussion Starters

- Read John 9 and Mark 7 with your student.

- When someone can't hear, they can use sign language to communicate with others. Look up sign language for the alphabet or certain phrases you use a lot, like "I love you."

- When someone can't see, they can read with their fingertips. Look up information on Braille and show your student the Braille alphabet.

Experience

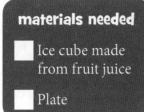

materials needed

☐ Ice cube made from fruit juice

☐ Plate

Today, we're going to use our five senses. Are you ready to get started?

Activity directions:

	teacher	ask student...
1. see	Place the ice cube on a plate. Ask your student to describe what they see. If your student likes to draw, he or she can also draw what they see.	What do you see?
	Ask which of their five senses they are using to view the ice cube.	
2. feel	Next, ask your student to feel the ice cube.	What does it feel like? Is it cold, hard, wet, slippery, bumpy, rough, smooth, etc.?
	Ask your student which of their five senses helps them know this.	
3. hear	Now instruct your student to put their ear close to the ice cube. Can they hear anything?	Is the ice cube silent or does it sound fizzy or crackly as it begins to melt?
	Ask your student which of their five senses helps them know the answer.	
4. smell	After listening closely, direct your student to smell the ice cube. Do they smell anything?	What does it smell like?
	Ask your student which of their five senses helps them know the answer.	
5. taste	Finally, have your student pick up the ice cube and lick it.	What does it taste like? What do they think the ice cube is made out of?
	Ask your student which of their five senses helps them know the answer.	

That was fun to use our five senses to discover what the ice cube looked like, felt like, sounded like, smelled like, and tasted like! Our five senses are great tools to help us explore, learn about, and discover the world God made!

Discussion Starters

Can you tell me about your five senses?

Can you think of something else you can explore with your five senses?

How do your five senses also help to protect you?

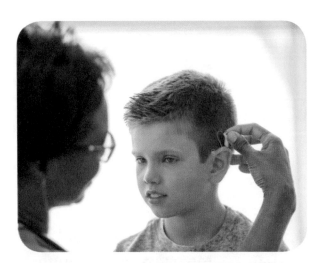

Day

Share

name

Wow, our five senses sure are neat tools God gave our bodies to explore the world around us! It's time to share what we've learned about our five senses and add a new page to our Science Notebook!

Draw a picture of something you can feel, see, taste, hear, or smell in the space.

1 **I can feel...**

2 **I can see...**

3 **I can taste...**

4 **I can hear...**

5 **I can smell...**

Trace the words and color the pictures

God gave us five tools
to help us learn and
explore, our five
senses!

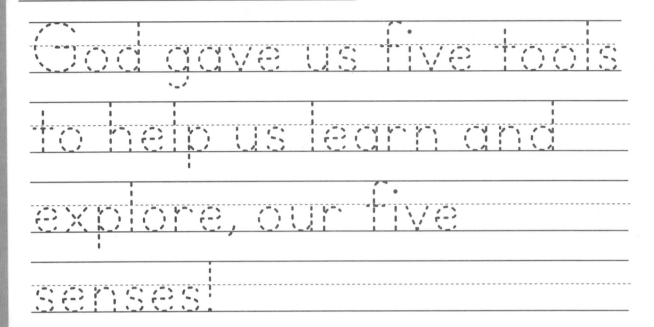

touch   hear   smell

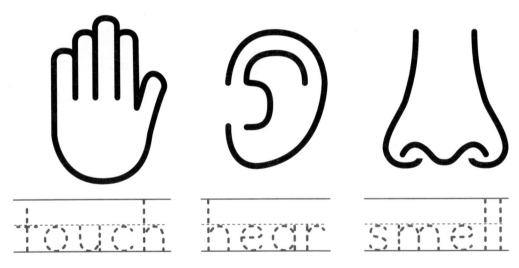

taste   see

Conclusion

7th Day of Creation—God rested.

Day

Learn

What an adventure we've had through the days of creation as we've studied God's world through science! At the start of our adventure, we learned what God created on the first day of creation. Do you remember what it was? God made the heavens, earth, and light. We learned that light travels fast, is made of colors, and travels in waves. We also learned about the rainbow.

Then we explored the second day of creation. Do you remember what God created on day two? The atmosphere! We learned about the layers of the atmosphere, about condensation and evaporation, clouds, the water cycle, and thunderstorms! What was your favorite?

Next came the third day, when God made dry land and plants. We explored continents, the layers of the earth, plants, photosynthesis, pollination, and seeds! Do you remember anything special from those science adventures?

What day came next? It was the fourth day, when God created the sun, moon, and stars! We learned some amazing things about the sun, the moon's surface and phases, and about stars and constellations. What do you think of when you look at the night sky now?

| Scissors | ✓ |
| Glue stick | ☐ |

Weekly materials list

Then we learned about the fifth day of creation, when God made birds and sea creatures. We discovered the design God gave bird feathers, how birds fly, and how they build their nests. Next, we explored the zones of the oceans and the sea creatures that live there.

Finally, we learned about the sixth day of creation, when God made animals and mankind. We learned about animal kinds and habitats, the respiratory system, the circulatory system, your fingerprint, and your five senses. Whew — we've learned a lot about God's creation this year!

It has also been fun to use our imaginations to visualize things Adam, Eve, Cain, and Abel may have experienced and talked about together. That reminds me — it's time to use our imaginations for one more story! Are you ready?

Bible-inspired stories

It was early in the morning, and a strange noise woke up both Cain and Abel. They were used to hearing the rooster crow outside early in the morning, but this sound was different. It sounded like a tiny cry.

Abel rubbed his tired eyes, and Cain yawned a big yawn. "What was that?" Abel whispered to Cain.

"Let's go find out!" Cain replied quietly.

Before they could get up, Adam came to them and whispered, "Boys, come with me! I want to show you something special!" There was another tiny cry as the boys hurried from their beds to follow Adam. He led them to their mom, Eve. She was holding a small bundle. The boys were very curious!

Eve smiled. "Boys," she said as another tiny cry came from the bundle in her arms,

"God has blessed us. Meet your baby sister!"

Eve pulled back the cloth to reveal the small baby in her arms. The baby had pudgy little cheeks and a lot of hair. The boys stepped closer to look. They were so very excited!

"A baby sister!" they both exclaimed.

Abel looked at Cain and whispered, "We sure have a lot to teach her about God's creation." They could hardly wait to tell their new baby sister about all the things they had learned.

· ·

The Bible tells us about real people like Adam and Eve, Cain and Abel, and others just like us who had a choice to make every day: Would they follow God's directions or not? Adam and Eve made the choice in the Garden of Eden to disobey God's directions. They sinned, and their sin broke God's perfect world. While we still see God's amazing design and mercy in creation, we also see a lot of sickness, sadness, pain, and death because of sin.

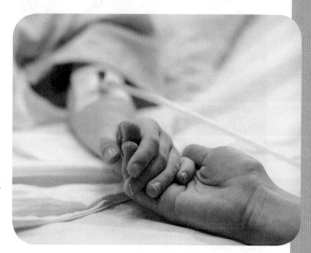

The Bible tells us about many different men and women. Some followed God's ways. They were not perfect, but they did their very best to follow God, and asked for His forgiveness when they made mistakes. Others did not follow God's ways. They made bad decisions that hurt themselves, other people, and hurt the heart of God. Later on, in Genesis, the Bible tells us that when Cain grew up, he decided not to follow God's directions. Not following God's directions is called sin. Sin hurts us, it hurts other people, and it separates us from God. It's a very sad thing.

When we study God's creation through science, we see His creativity, organization, grace, mercy, and majesty on display in everything. The things we learn through science remind us that God is amazing, that He cares for us, that He loves us, and that He has mercy on us. It also reminds us that sin broke the world, and we have a choice. Will we follow God's directions or not? I'm so glad God's plan wasn't over when Adam and Eve sinned. God sent Jesus to pay the price of sin for us. We can trust Jesus and grow in our faith in Him.

Remember the verse we read at the very beginning of our science adventure? Psalm 111:2–4 tells us, *"Great are the works of the LORD; they are pondered by all who delight in them. Glorious and majestic are his deeds, and his righteousness endures forever. He has caused his wonders to be remembered; the LORD is gracious and compassionate."*

We've learned about some of God's great works, and you're going to have many more science adventures as you learn and grow. There are lots of things to learn about God's creation and about Him as you continue to study science. Ready for some fun?

name

Draw each day of creation!

1 Light & Dark

2 Sky

3 Dry Land, Plants, Seas

4 Stars, Moon, Sun

5 Birds, Sea Life

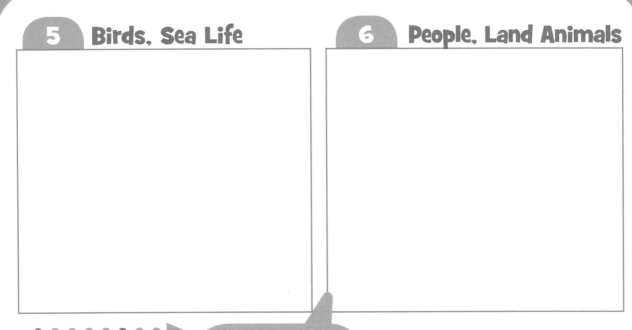

6 People, Land Animals

Discussion Starters

Read Genesis 1.

Can you tell me about a time you made the choice to follow God's directions?

What would you like to learn about next?

Ooh, wait — you thought we were all done, didn't you? Well, there was actually one more day of creation — the seventh day! What do you think God did on the seventh day? Let's read from Genesis 2:1–3 to find out:

Experience

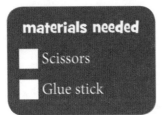

materials needed

- [ ] Scissors
- [ ] Glue stick

Thus the heavens and the earth were completed in all their vast array. By the seventh day God had finished the work he had been doing; so on the seventh day he rested from all his work. Then God blessed the seventh day and made it holy, because on it he rested from all the work of creating that he had done.

Did you hear our answer? I think I heard it, too. On the seventh day of creation, God rested. For six days, God created, and on the seventh day, He rested. Hmm, that sounds like our week, doesn't it? We work for six days, and on the seventh day, we rest and worship God. God created the week, too!

Let's see if we can remember what God created on the six days!

Activity directions:

1. Help your student cut out the days of creation images below.

2. Arrange the images on the worksheet on page 341 in order, then glue them down.

3. You can give hints and help your student as needed. The order is:

Day 1: Light, heavens, and the earth
Day 2: Atmosphere
Day 3: Land and plants
Day 4: Sun, moon, and stars
Day 5: Birds and sea creatures
Day 6: Animals and mankind

Blank for cutting out creation cards.

name

Days of Creation

Discussion Starters

Can you tell me about the days of creation?

What was your favorite thing to learn about?

What did God do on the seventh day?

name

Congratulations, you've made it to the end of this adventure, and you've learned so much!

Share It's time to add one last page to our Science Notebook. You're a certified science explorer now! You've learned all about the days of creation, and you've learned how to share what you've learned about science and about God with others. Let's add your science explorer certification to your Science Notebook!

Do you remember Psalm 111:2? We learned that verse at the very start of our science adventure. Let's say it together!

Let's memorize
Psalm 111:2

"**Great** are the **works** of the **LORD**; they are **pondered** by **all** who **delight** in them."

	Actions
Great	Place both hands in front of you over your head. Palms will face out like they would in a "stop" signal.
works	Make your hands into fists — one on the bottom, one on top. Tap your top fist onto the bottom fist.
LORD	Make an L with your pointer finger and thumb on your left hand. Place your L hand at your right shoulder and cross it in front of you to your left hip — almost like you are wearing a sash and tracing over it with your hand. You can also search for this sign online to see it in action by searching "sign language for Lord."
pondered	Tap your forehead as if you are thinking.
all	Sweep your hands around the room as if gesturing to a large crowd of people.
delight	Hold hands palm up and raise them to about eye level.

Certified Science Explorer

_____

name

_____

Signature

_____

Date

Blank for certificate.

Language Lessons for a Living Education

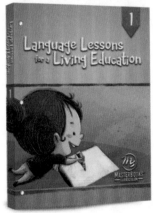

GRADE 1
LANGUAGE LESSONS FOR A LIVING EDUCATION 1

978-1-68344-211-0

GRADE 2
LANGUAGE LESSONS FOR A LIVING EDUCATION 2

978-1-68344-122-9

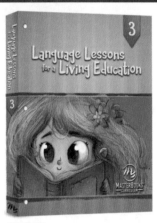

GRADE 3
LANGUAGE LESSONS FOR A LIVING EDUCATION 3

978-1-68344-137-3

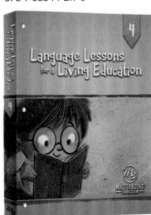

GRADE 4
LANGUAGE LESSONS FOR A LIVING EDUCATION 4

978-1-68344-138-0

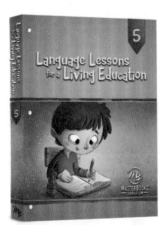

GRADE 5
LANGUAGE LESSONS FOR A LIVING EDUCATION 5

978-1-68344-178-6

GRADE 6
LANGUAGE LESSONS FOR A LIVING EDUCATION 6

978-1-68344-209-7

LEVELS K-6
MATH LESSONS FOR A LIVING EDUCATION
A CHARLOTTE MASON FLAVOR TO MATH FOR TODAY'S STUDENT

Level K, Kindergarten
978-1-68344-176-2

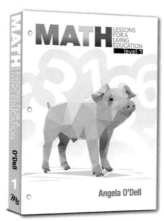

Level 1, Grade 1
978-0-89051-923-3

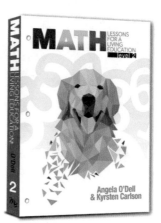

Level 2, Grade 2
978-0-89051-924-0

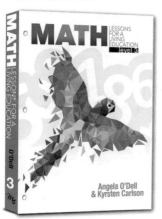

Level 3, Grade 3
978-0-89051-925-7

Level 4, Grade 4
978-0-89051-926-4

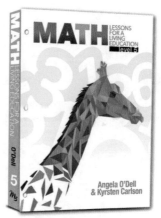

Level 5, Grade 5
978-0-89051-927-1

ATTRACTIVE FULL-COLOR LESSONS

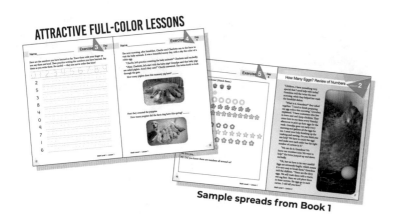

Sample spreads from Book 1

Level 6, Grade 6
978-1-68344-024-6

My Story

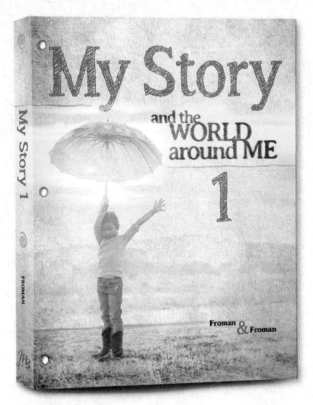

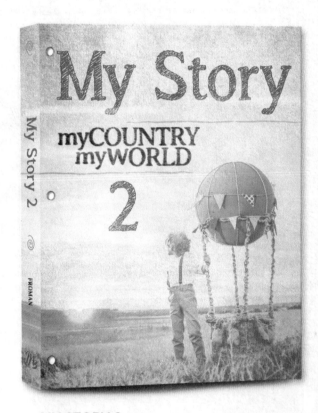

MY STORY 1
GRADE 1

This level one Social Studies Curriculum begins with children in their homes, helping them think about their lives from their immediate families and beyond, as well as learning about local governments. Includes four quests.

9781683441175

MY STORY 2
GRADE 2

This level two Social Studies Curriculum continues with a journey around the world, and lays a foundation for understanding state and federal governments, basic economic principles, and more. Four global quests included.

9781683441182

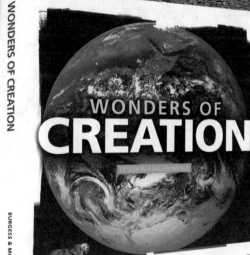